Playing With Fire

The Redhead Experience

Amanda Blackwood

MANDOLIN PUBLISHING

PUBLISHED BY THE MANDOLIN PUBLISHING GROUP

Introduction

Growing up as a natural redhead in a world that seemed to celebrate blending in was quite the rollercoaster ride. Imagine this: bright red hair, fair skin splattered with freckles, and a personality still trying to find its footing. From an early age, my hair was like a neon sign shouting, "Look at me!" while all I wanted was to blend into the crowd. Instead, I became the target of relentless bullying.

Kids can be cruel, and I was no exception to their inventive meanness. They'd taunt me with names like "fire crotch," their laughter ringing in my ears like an annoying pop song stuck on repeat. I vividly remember one particularly harsh winter day, bundled in my oversized coat, feeling every bit the outcast as I trudged through the school hallway. The whispers followed me like an unwanted shadow. What I hoped would be a source of magic instead became a source of pain.

For years, I tried to hide my vibrant locks, wishing I could melt into the background like everyone else. I kept my hair tucked under hats and opted for dark colors to avoid standing out even more. At fifteen, my mother, who "always hated" my hair color, decided to bleach it. The result? A vibrant carrot orange. It wasn't until my mid-20s that I began to embrace the wild, fiery hair I was born with—though I went a little overboard with unnaturally bright dyes. After all, if you're going to be a target, you might as well do it in style, right? I dove into a world of vibrant dyes, outrageous hairstyles, and outfits that would make any stereotype come alive. Suddenly, I wasn't just a redhead; I was *the* redhead—loud, proud, and fully embracing every exaggerated trait thrown my way. It even landed me roles on several TV shows.

That's when the magic started. In a moment of whimsy and a desire for connection, I created a Facebook group called Redhead Memes in 2017. I thought, why not gather some funny posts about the absurdities of being a redhead? To my astonishment, the group exploded overnight. Within days, hundreds of people were sharing their experiences and laughter, along with a treasure trove of memes perfectly encapsulating the redhead experience. I suddenly found myself part of a community that celebrated what I had once tried to hide. The group soon grew to over 50,000 members who bonded over our shared experiences.

Before long, the group morphed into the popular "Redhead Memes & Things" page—a haven for redheads (and those who appreciated their fiery spirit) to gather, share, and find humor in our unique struggles. What began as a small gathering turned into a booming community filled with laughter, support, and a healthy dose of sarcasm.

Through this journey, I learned that my experiences, while painful, were far from unique. The bullying, stereotypes, and even the occasional envy from non-redheads became fuel for inside jokes and camaraderie. It marked the beginning of something incredible—a place where redheads could celebrate our uniqueness rather than hide it.

As the group thrived, I found myself not just sharing my own experiences but becoming part of something larger—a community of people who understood the ups and downs of having red hair. Each day brought new posts: memes that made me laugh until I cried, stories that echoed my own, and photos of redheads flaunting their fiery locks like badges of honor. It felt like a family reunion where everyone just happened to be fabulously redheaded.

The diversity within the group was astonishing. Redheads from all walks of life shared their unique experiences. Some, like me, had dealt with bullying, while others had worn their hair with pride from day one. There were those who embraced their red locks as a symbol of individuality and others still on the journey of acceptance. The camaraderie was palpable; we were all in this together, whether swapping tales of sunburned noses or the absurdity of explaining our hair color for the hundredth time.

One day, as I scrolled through the group, I came across a post from a member describing her struggles with self-esteem, feeling like her red hair set her apart in a world that often celebrated conformity. Her words resonated with me, prompting me to share my own story—how the bullying had made me feel small and how it took years to find my confidence. The response was overwhelming; messages poured in, filled with gratitude and shared experiences. It was then I realized the power of connection and the relief of knowing you're not alone in your struggles.

Inspired by this wave of support, I began organizing virtual events where redheads could chat, share hair care tips, and swap stories. We laughed over the ridiculous things people say about redheads and bonded over our mutual love for our fiery hair. I even introduced themed weeks like "Fierce Redhead Fashion" and "Fabulous Freckles," where members showcased their unique styles and celebrated their individuality.

Before long, the "Redhead Memes and Things" page became a go-to spot for redheads everywhere, catching the attention of brands and influencers who reached out for collaborations. What started as a small Facebook group blossomed into a vibrant platform that celebrated our fiery hair and quirky personalities. Messages from non-redheads who simply loved the humor and spirit of the page flooded in, thanking us for offering a glimpse into the redhead experience.

One of my proudest moments came when we organized a charity event to raise awareness for bullying prevention. The response was heartwarming; members donated their time, talents, and resources to create a virtual fundraiser. It was empowering to see our community transform from a group of individuals into a collective force for good. We were using our shared experiences to make a positive impact in the world, turning pain into purpose.

Reflecting on this whirlwind of community-building, I realized I was no longer the timid kid hiding her hair under a hat. I had grown into a confident redhead, fully embracing my uniqueness and encouraging others to do the same. The laughter we shared, the support we offered, and the stories we told fueled my desire to create something even bigger—a book that captured the essence of what it means to be a natural redhead.

It dawned on me that this journey wasn't just mine; it belonged to every redhead who ever felt out of place, every person bullied for their appearance, and every individual who learned to love themselves against all odds. Writing this book was my way to honor those experiences, weaving together the collective tapestry of redheaded life and inspiring others to embrace their unique identities.

So here I am, years later, on this exciting adventure of writing *Playing with Fire: The Redhead Experience* as a tribute to all those fiery-haired souls out there. The journey from shame to pride was long, but it ultimately led to a sense of belonging that I had always craved. With each chapter, I hope to shine a light on the humor, challenges, and downright absurdities of life as a redhead. Whether you have flaming locks, envy them from afar, or just appreciate a good story, I invite you to join me on this journey of self-discovery, laughter, and fiery spirit. Let's dive deeper into what it truly means to play with fire.

Genetics of Red Hair

When it comes to hair color, red is like the rock star of the hair world—rare, bold, and just a tad unpredictable, kind of like a cat on a hot tin roof. But what exactly makes some of us redheads? The answer lies in the fascinating realm of genetics, a tale that intertwines biology, evolution, and a generous splash of luck—like finding a four-leaf clover in a field of dandelions.

At the heart of our fiery locks is a gene known as MC1R. This little powerhouse is responsible for the production of melanin, the pigment that determines the color of our hair, skin, and eyes. Most people have a mix of two types of melanin: eumelanin (which is dark, much like the depths of your ex's soul) and pheomelanin (which is lighter and gives us those lovely shades of red and yellow). In redheads, the MC1R gene takes the stage like a diva at a karaoke bar, shifting the balance heavily in favor of pheomelanin. Essentially, our hair ends up being a brilliant shade of red because we have less melanin in the mix. You could say we're the delicate soufflés of the hair color world—light, airy, and prone to collapse under pressure!

But it's not just a simple case of "one gene equals one color." Oh no, the genetics of red hair is a bit more complex than that. Variations in the MC1R gene can lead to different shades of red, from the deep auburn that looks like it belongs in a Renaissance painting to the bright copper that practically screams, "Look at me!" Each redhead is like a walking, talking color palette, and every head of fiery hair tells a unique story. It's like a hair color buffet, and we're all picking different dishes!

So, where did this fiery trait come from? Well, red hair is often linked to ancestry, particularly in Celtic regions like Ireland and Scotland. In fact, it's estimated that about 10% of people with Irish heritage have red hair, while Scotland boasts the highest percentage of redheads per capita in the world. It's as if these regions put up a big neon "Welcome, Gingers!" sign, creating a culture that celebrates and cherishes this rarity. If you ever find yourself in a pub in Dublin, just look for the redheads; it's like finding the pot of gold at the end of the rainbow! And let's be honest—there's nothing quite like sharing a pint with someone who understands your hair-related struggles.

But wait—there's more! Evolutionary biologists have speculated that red hair may have developed as a survival adaptation. It's believed that the lighter skin often accompanying red hair evolved to help individuals absorb more sunlight and produce vitamin D in regions with less sunlight. So, in a way, being a redhead is like having a clever evolutionary hack. Who knew our fiery manes could be linked to our health? It's like Mother Nature threw us a bone—"You may burn like a lobster in the sun, but at least you can soak up those rays like a champ!"

Now, let's talk about the numbers. Redheads are among the rarest of hair colors, making up only about 1-2% of the global population. That's a small club! To put it into perspective, there are more people with naturally blonde hair than red. This rarity is what makes red hair so special and sought after, often leading to a delightful mix of admiration and envy. If I had a dime for every time someone exclaimed, "I'd kill for your hair," I could probably fund a small island getaway, or at least afford a lifetime supply of hair products to keep my locks looking fabulous!

Of course, with such uniqueness comes a whirlwind of attention. From curious kids in school to adults in the workplace, redheads often find themselves at the center of fascination—and sometimes unwarranted scrutiny. The questions can range from the innocent ("How did you get your hair that color?") to the downright bizarre ("Do you have a special diet to keep your hair so vibrant?"). I mean, sure, I'd love to reveal my secret: it involves a carefully curated blend of sunlight, good vibes, and maybe a little magic—preferably from a fairy godmother.

Then there are the comments that feel like a double-edged sword. "Is your hair real?" they ask, as if I'm some sort of walking exhibit in a museum of natural wonders. Or the classic, "You know, redheads have fiery tempers!" Oh, do we? Because I thought my temper was just a natural response to being asked the same ridiculous questions over and over again! At some point, we could start a "Redhead FAQ" just to streamline the conversation.

The beauty of understanding the science behind red hair is that it allows us to appreciate it on a deeper level. We're not just walking punchlines or stereotypes; we're the result of a complex interplay of genetics and evolution. Each strand of our hair tells a story that connects us to our ancestors and our environment. So the next time someone asks how I got my hair color, I might just respond with, "It's a long story involving ancient Celts, a dash of sunlight, and maybe a little luck."

This journey of understanding doesn't just stop with the science; it dives into our social interactions, our perceptions of beauty, and the community we create around our uniqueness. We redheads have a bond, a shared experience that transcends geography and background. We may have different shades, but our collective identity sparkles just as brightly.

So, as we celebrate our fiery locks and navigate the world, let's remember that being a redhead isn't just about how we look—it's about the stories we carry, the laughter we share, and the community we build. In a world where blending in often feels like the norm, we redheads stand out—and that's a badge of honor worth flaunting!

Myths and Misconceptions

Red hair has captivated human imagination for centuries, stirring up a rich tapestry of myths, misconceptions, and cultural narratives that range from the whimsical to the downright bizarre. Throughout history, redheads have been portrayed in various ways—often based on superstition, folklore, and a deep-seated fascination with their unique appearance. This essay explores the historical myths and misconceptions surrounding redheads, examining how they have been perceived across different cultures and time periods. Spoiler alert: it's not all sunshine and rainbows (or fiery manes).

The myths surrounding red hair can be traced back to ancient civilizations, where it seems everyone had an opinion about it—much like a family dinner where Aunt Gertrude insists on discussing your dating life. In ancient Egypt, for example, redheads were considered a sign of the divine, often associated with the god Set, who was depicted with red hair. So, if you were rocking a red 'do back then, you were either favored by the gods or destined to start some serious chaos—no pressure, right?

In Greco-Roman society, red hair was similarly imbued with mystique. The Roman poet Ovid described red-haired people as fiery and passionate, suggesting a temperament that was quick to anger and prone to fierce emotions. This stereotype of redheads as hot-headed has persisted throughout history, reinforcing the idea that red hair is linked to uncontrollable emotions. So if you ever find yourself accused of overreacting, just remember: it's not you, it's the hair!

The medieval period saw a surge in the demonization of redheads—because what's a good witch hunt without a few fiery-haired suspects? During the Inquisition, red hair became synonymous with witchcraft and the supernatural. Women with red hair were often scrutinized, and many were accused of witchcraft simply because of their hair color. Yes, apparently all you needed to do to be labeled a witch was to stand in a light breeze while sporting a killer mane of red. If only they knew it took an entire bottle of conditioner to maintain that shine!

During the Renaissance, the perception of redheads began to shift slightly, but not entirely for the better. While red hair was sometimes celebrated in art—think of the beautiful Titian-haired maidens painted by Titian and Botticelli—it was also seen as a marker of moral ambiguity. In Shakespeare's plays, red-haired characters often embody strong and complex emotions, reflecting the cultural duality surrounding red hair. It's almost like Shakespeare had a redhead friend and thought, "Why not make them both the heroine and the villain? Talk about drama!"

The 19th century brought about more nuanced views of redheads, especially in literature and art. Writers like Edgar Allan Poe and Nathaniel Hawthorne featured red-haired characters, often imbuing them with a sense of mystery and otherworldliness. However, this fascination was not without its pitfalls. The stereotype of the "fiery redhead" emerged, depicting red-haired women as seductive yet unpredictable. Just imagine: "She's beautiful, passionate, and likely to throw a lamp at you. Date at your own risk!"

By the 20th century, red hair had begun to be seen through a more romantic lens. Iconic figures like Lucille Ball, Anne of Green Gables, and other cultural icons helped shift perceptions. While redheads were still often characterized by their fiery personalities, they also became symbols of independence and strength. Yet, the underlying stereotypes remained intact; the idea of the "crazy redhead" still lingered, suggesting that passion could easily tip into madness. Who knew that the secret to redhead charm was a pinch of madness and a dash of charisma?

In contemporary society, redheads still navigate a complex web of myths and misconceptions. A prevalent stereotype suggests that redheads are more aggressive or confrontational than their non-redheaded counterparts. This idea has been perpetuated by media representations, where red-haired characters often embody fiery tempers or rebellious spirits. While these portrayals can be empowering, they can also pigeonhole redheads into narrow, exaggerated roles. "She's got red hair—better not ask her where she wants to eat!"

Additionally, there are misconceptions about red hair itself. Some believe that redheads have a lower pain threshold or that they are more likely to be fiery and irritable. Scientific studies have debunked these myths, showing that hair color does not determine personality traits or physical responses to pain. But if someone tells you that redheads have an extra chromosome that makes them more fabulous, don't question it; just roll with it!

As society evolves, the understanding of redheads and their diverse experiences continues to grow. While historical myths and misconceptions have shaped perceptions of red hair, they are not definitive. Many modern redheads are reclaiming their identity, embracing their hair color as a badge of honor rather than a source of shame. Social media platforms have created spaces for redheads to celebrate their uniqueness, sharing stories, humor, and solidarity. So, if you're ever feeling down about your hair color, just remember: you're not just a redhead; you're a walking legend!

The historical myths and misconceptions surrounding redheads reveal much about societal attitudes toward difference and individuality. From ancient civilizations to modern representations, red hair has sparked curiosity, admiration, and even fear. While some stereotypes may linger, the journey of redheads is a testament to resilience, highlighting the importance of embracing one's identity amidst a tapestry of cultural narratives. The future promises a richer understanding of what it means to be a redhead, one that transcends old myths and celebrates the vibrant, fiery spirit that comes with the color. And if all else fails, just remember: red hair is basically the universe's way of saying, "You're fabulous—now go own it!"

The Color Spectrum of Red

Just as no two redheads are alike, no two shades of red are identical. This chapter will unpack the intricacies of hair pigmentation, revealing how genetics creates a vibrant palette of fiery hues. So buckle up—it's going to be a colorful ride!

First, let's take a look at the varying shades of red hair. From deep auburn that looks like it was brewed in a mysterious pot of magic to bright strawberry blonde that could make a summer sunset jealous, the spectrum is both rich and varied. The differences come from the interplay of genetics, particularly the variations within the MC1R gene. While we all produce pheomelanin, the intensity and ratio of this pigment can vary widely, resulting in everything from the soft, golden tones of a strawberry blonde to the rich, dark depths of a mahogany red. It's like a box of crayons, except that these crayons are alive and full of sass!

Interestingly, some redheads can also have a mix of eumelanin in their hair, albeit in lesser amounts. This blend can create unique shades, making it difficult for even the most experienced hair colorist to replicate. Imagine the look on a stylist's face when you request "sunset on a rainy day" and they have to squint at your hair like it's a riddle wrapped in an enigma. This genetic variation leads to that delightful surprise we sometimes find in our locks: a hidden shimmer that catches the light just right, creating a sparkling effect that seems to dance when we move. We're basically walking disco balls—just without the music and with a bit more freckling!

But it's not just genetics that influences our hair color. Environmental factors, such as sun exposure and hair care routines, also play a role. For example, spending time in the sun can lighten red hair, bringing out those golden or copper undertones. You could say that redheads have a built-in highlight feature—who needs salon appointments when you can just bake yourself under the sun like a cookie? On the flip side, harsh hair products or frequent dyeing can dull the vibrancy of those precious red strands, making it essential for us to choose our products wisely. We need to treat our hair like royalty—because, honestly, it deserves nothing less!

Now, let's talk about how society perceives these various shades. Redheads have often been romanticized in art and literature, portrayed as fiery and passionate characters. Think of the iconic depictions of red-haired figures like Anne of Green Gables or the stunning Sirens of folklore. These representations celebrate the beauty and uniqueness of red hair, yet they also perpetuate certain stereotypes that can be both flattering and frustrating. I mean, yes, I can be passionate, but that doesn't mean I'm going to throw a tantrum every time I run out of my favorite hair product—though it might come close!

For example, redheads are often associated with fiery tempers or rebellious spirits, a trope that can lead to expectations that feel impossible to live up to. One minute you're enjoying a quiet afternoon, and the next, someone's reminding you that you're supposed to be a tempestuous force of nature. On the other hand, we also embody a sense of rarity and allure, which can make us the center of attention—both wanted and unwanted. Imagine walking into a room and feeling like a rare bird in a flock of pigeons—everyone's eyes are on you, and you can't decide whether to revel in the spotlight or just find the nearest exit!

But fear not! Understanding these societal perceptions can help us navigate our identities as redheads and take pride in the varied shades that define us. With our hair color comes an implicit challenge to defy norms and embrace our individuality. After all, when you stand out in a crowd, you're also in a prime position to make an entrance. Just think of yourself as the main character in a rom-com—there's bound to be some mischief and a few awkward moments, but at least you're the one in the spotlight!

Now, let's not forget the science behind hair care products specifically formulated for red hair. Many brands have developed shampoos, conditioners, and styling products aimed at preserving and enhancing the vibrancy of our fiery locks. These products often contain ingredients designed to combat fading and maintain the color's intensity. From UV protection to color-lock technology, the market caters to the unique needs of redheads, giving us the tools to shine even brighter. Because if we're going to stand out, we might as well do it in style!

In the age of social media, where beauty standards are constantly evolving, there's been a recent trend of redhead appreciation. Platforms like Instagram are filled with accounts dedicated to celebrating red hair, showcasing everything from bold styling choices to daily routines that keep those locks looking radiant. This wave of positivity is a welcome shift, allowing redheads to connect, share tips, and support one another in a community that champions our uniqueness. It's like a never-ending pep rally, complete with virtual high-fives and lots of flaming hair emojis.

The spectrum of red hair is as diverse as the individuals who wear it. Each shade tells a story rooted in genetics, culture, and personal expression. There's something magical about knowing that your hair color links you to a long line of history and tradition. It's as if every fiery strand carries a piece of heritage, whispering secrets from our ancestors who also stood out in their own ways—perhaps dodging the same questions about "What do you feed your hair to keep it so bright?"

As we continue to explore the world of redheads in the following chapters, we'll dive into the myths, historical significance, and the ongoing journey of self-acceptance that accompanies being a natural redhead. Let's embrace our fiery heritage and celebrate the dazzling array of colors that make us who we are! So grab your favorite hair product, strike a pose, and let's show the world just how vibrant red can be. Together, we'll flaunt our unique shades, share a few laughs, and maybe even debunk some myths along the way. After all, who said being a redhead was anything less than a full-time job of fabulousness?

The Rarity of Red

Hair color is one of the most noticeable traits we possess, influencing how we see ourselves and how others see us. Among the myriad shades found in nature—blonde, brunette, black, and gray—red hair stands out as the rarest and most intriguing. It's like the rare Pokémon of hair colors—everyone wants to catch it, but only a few have the lucky cards! But what exactly determines our hair color? Spoiler alert: the answer lies in the complex interplay of genetics and pigments, primarily melanin.

Melanin is a natural pigment produced by specialized cells called melanocytes, located in the hair follicles, skin, and eyes. It serves several functions, but its most notable role is in determining color. There are two main types of melanin: eumelanin (the dark, brooding type responsible for black and brown hair) and pheomelanin (the lighter, sunnier type that gives us those fabulous shades of red and yellow). The ratio of these two types of melanin dictates not just our hair color, but also aspects of our skin tone and even our eye color. So, in a way, our hair is like a mood ring—only instead of changing colors based on our feelings, it changes based on our genetic lottery!

In the case of red hair, there is a distinctive predominance of pheomelanin. This unique composition not only defines the vibrant hues associated with redheads but also influences other traits, like skin sensitivity to sunlight. Red hair often comes hand-in-hand with lighter skin, which contains less eumelanin. This delightful combo means redheads are more susceptible to sunburn—perfect for those of us who've always wanted to be human barometers!

The production of melanin is a complex process controlled by various genes, with the most critical being the MC1R gene. Located on chromosome 16, this gene encodes a receptor that's essential for converting pheomelanin to eumelanin. When the MC1R gene is functioning normally, it promotes a harmonious balance between these two types of melanin. However, specific mutations in this gene can throw a wrench in the works, leading to a reduced ability to produce eumelanin. The result? A glorious riot of red hair that turns heads and sparks questions like, "Is that your natural color, or did you lose a bet?"

Understanding the basics of hair color is vital for grasping the genetic underpinnings of red hair. It's essential to realize that hair color isn't just an aesthetic feature; it's a trait intricately woven into the fabric of our genetics. The interplay of environmental factors and genetic variations creates a rich tapestry that defines not only red hair but also the uniqueness of each individual. Just think of it as nature's way of keeping things interesting!

At the heart of the red hair phenomenon lies the MC1R gene, the unsung hero of the hair color saga. Understanding this gene is essential for unraveling the mysteries behind why some individuals are born with those striking red locks while others are not. The MC1R gene, or "melanocortin 1 receptor," is like the backstage pass that lets us see how hair color is produced.

Interestingly, the MC1R gene isn't just about hair color; it also influences other traits, like skin tone and sensitivity to sunlight. Redheads often have fair skin with less eumelanin, making them more susceptible to sunburn and skin damage. It's almost like Mother Nature said, "You can have fabulous hair, but you'll need to carry sunscreen everywhere!" This connection between the MC1R gene and skin characteristics underscores the importance of this gene beyond just hair color.

One of the most fascinating aspects of the MC1R gene is its role in evolution. Research suggests that the gene's variants may have provided advantages in specific environments, particularly in northern latitudes with lower UV radiation. Having lighter skin allows for more efficient vitamin D synthesis, which is essential for overall health. So, in a way, the MC1R gene is like a well-traveled guide, showing us how to adapt and thrive in different climates. Who knew that red hair could be a savvy evolutionary hack?

Despite the genetic basis for red hair, the variations of the MC1R gene that lead to this trait can be quite diverse. Some variants are more common in certain populations, resulting in different shades of red hair—from strawberry blonde to deep auburn. This diversity adds a layer of richness to the redhead experience, making each of us a unique shade on the vibrant palette of life. It's like a crayon box where every redhead is a different hue, but we all share that same spicy essence!

In addition to its aesthetic implications, the MC1R gene has also caught the attention of scientists. Studies have explored its connection to pain sensitivity and the body's response to certain medications. Redheads, for example, have been found to experience pain differently—probably because our fiery nature makes us tough cookies! This discovery highlights the multifaceted role of the MC1R gene in human biology. Who knew our hair color could come with a side of science?

As we delve deeper into the genetics of red hair, it becomes clear that the MC1R gene is not merely a switch that turns red hair on or off. Instead, it's part of a complex web of genetic interactions that shape not only hair color but also a range of physical characteristics. The influence of this gene stretches beyond appearance, connecting with aspects of health, evolutionary biology, and even pain perception. Talk about a multitasking gene—it should get a medal for all that it does!

Childhood Flames

From the moment I first set foot in a classroom, my bright red hair seemed to have a life of its own. It was like a neon sign that said, "Look at me! I'm fabulous!" While many kids might have wished for the unassuming nature of brown or blonde locks, my fiery mane was both a source of fascination and a catalyst for discomfort. In a world where fitting in often felt like the ultimate goal, standing out became a double-edged sword—sort of like trying to use a sword to cut your hair.

As a child, I loved the attention that came from my hair. I remember the first time a teacher complimented me, her voice full of admiration. "What a beautiful color!" she exclaimed, and my chest puffed up with pride, like a peacock in a flock of pigeons. But as the school year rolled on, that admiration quickly morphed into something more complicated—kind of like how a cute puppy can turn into a drooling monster when it's hungry.

"Ginger!" "Carrot top!" These nicknames began to echo through the hallways, often accompanied by laughter that pierced my heart like a poorly aimed dart. At first, I tried to laugh along, thinking it was all in good fun. But with each passing day, the teasing grew sharper, more cutting. It became clear that not everyone saw my hair as a beautiful anomaly; for some, it was the perfect target practice. What started as innocent curiosity quickly devolved into a chorus of mockery that left me feeling as isolated as a lone sock in a dryer.

Navigating the complexities of social dynamics as a redhead was particularly challenging. Kids can be wonderfully imaginative, but they can also be painfully straightforward. My hair became a topic of constant discussion—more often than not, a punchline rather than a compliment. I recall one lunch period where a group of classmates gathered around, eagerly sharing their latest jokes. "Did you hear about the redhead who got lost in a cornfield?" one boy shouted, and the others erupted in laughter. The punchline—something about being too bright to hide—hit me like a slap in the face, or more accurately, like a corn stalk in the forehead.

In the midst of this attention, there were moments when I craved normalcy. I wanted to blend in, to be like everyone else, rather than the walking advertisement for "Look at me!" I began experimenting with hair ties and hats, desperate attempts to tone down my brightness. "If only I had brown hair," I'd mutter to myself, wishing for a color that would allow me to go unnoticed. It was a painful irony: my hair, which should have been a source of pride, felt more like a burden—like carrying around a piñata at a party where everyone was allergic to candy.

Family dynamics didn't help the situation either. My mother, who had her own complicated feelings about my red hair, often expressed her disappointment. "Why can't you just color it brown like everyone else?" she would say, as if my hair were an affront to her standards. Those comments cut deeper than a bad haircut, reinforcing my feelings of being different and unwanted. While other kids received encouragement and praise from their families, I often felt like an outsider in my own home—like the only person at a potluck who brought a salad when everyone else showed up with dessert.

Yet, despite the challenges, there were fleeting moments of joy that punctured the gloom. I remember a summer day spent in the backyard with my friends, the sun gleaming off my hair and creating a halo effect. We played games and laughed, and for a while, I forgot about the teasing. My hair shone bright, and in that moment, I felt like a princess in a fairy tale—one who, let's be honest, probably had a few trolls lurking around.

Through it all, I learned to cultivate a sense of humor as a coping mechanism. I remember one particularly tough day when a classmate made a snide remark about my hair. Instead of sinking into despair, I responded with a playful quip: "Yeah, but at least my hair has personality!" The laughter that followed felt like a small victory, a reminder that I could reclaim my narrative in my own way—one snappy comeback at a time.

Hair Raising Comments

Red hair has always captured attention, evoking a mix of admiration, curiosity, and sometimes, confusion—like trying to figure out why a cat would knock over a glass of water just to watch it spill. From ancient civilizations to modern society, this striking hue has woven itself into cultural narratives, becoming a symbol of beauty, individuality, and even mystique. In this chapter, we'll explore the historical perceptions of red hair, the compliments that often accompany it, and how these reactions can make a redhead feel like they're carrying a fabulous yet heavy crown—one that may or may not be made of fire.

Historically, red hair has been viewed through various lenses—sometimes flattering, other times resembling the way you might look at a weird art installation. In some cultures, it was celebrated as a mark of uniqueness, often linked to fiery personalities. The ancient Greeks believed red hair signified a fierce temper, while medieval Europe sometimes associated it with witchcraft. (So basically, they thought redheads were either passionate leaders or misunderstood sorceresses—good luck choosing between those career paths.) Despite the negative connotations, there were always those who recognized the beauty in this rare hue. Renaissance art even featured red-haired figures as symbols of vitality, capturing the essence of what it's like to be a living sunset—bright, bold, and slightly baffling to those who prefer beige.

Fast forward to today, and red hair continues to draw compliments that reflect its rarity. People often marvel at the vibrant hues, exclaiming, "Your hair is stunning!" or "I've always wanted to be a redhead!" For many redheads, this is the equivalent of receiving a gold star—until it starts to feel like a responsibility to be the embodiment of all things fiery. After all, only about 1-2% of the global population has naturally red hair, making it feel like you're in an exclusive club where the membership criteria mostly revolve around your hair color and a knack for dodging questions about your "natural" hue.

But let's face it: receiving compliments can be a double-edged sword. While some redheads bask in the glow of admiration, others may feel the pressure to be "the redhead"—a title that can overshadow their multifaceted personality. It's like being cast as the star of a one-woman show called "Look at My Hair!" while secretly wanting to perform a dramatic monologue about your deep love for existential philosophy.

Despite these complexities, the impact of positive reactions can't be overstated. Compliments can boost self-esteem and encourage individuals to embrace their natural beauty. Studies have shown that receiving affirmations about one's appearance can enhance self-image—so when someone admires your hair, it's like a little pep talk from the universe, reminding you that your uniqueness is something to be celebrated, not hidden away like a secret stash of Halloween candy.

The beauty of red hair lies not just in its color, but also in its ability to spark curiosity and conversation. People often feel compelled to ask questions: "Is it natural?" "What's your secret?" These inquiries, while sometimes intrusive (seriously, I don't walk around asking about your hair products, do I?), stem from genuine interest. For many redheads, these reactions create opportunities for connection, letting them share stories and engage with others—whether it's about hair care tips or how they're totally not actually related to that infamous fiery-haired character from that one movie.

As we navigate the spectrum of reactions to red hair, it's essential to recognize that beauty is subjective. While some might see red hair as a defining feature, others might see it as merely one part of a much larger tapestry—like an intriguing thread in a blanket that mostly features cats and coffee. Embracing this perspective allows for a richer understanding of individuality, encouraging all people—regardless of hair color—to celebrate their unique qualities.

Curiosity is a natural human trait, and red hair often acts as a magnet for questions and intrigue. For many redheads, the inquiries they face can range from innocent wonder to downright absurdity. I mean, who hasn't been asked, "Do you dye your eyebrows?" or "Does your hair change color in the sun?"—as if they have some magical ability to morph with the weather. While these questions can be amusing, they also highlight how red hair captivates the imagination, prompting people to consider the science behind it—like a real-life experiment gone delightfully awry.

Interactions driven by curiosity can create chances for connection. When approached with genuine interest, questions can lead to engaging conversations, allowing redheads to share their experiences—whether it's the struggles of finding the right shampoo or how they've been mistaken for a character from a cartoon. These moments can foster camaraderie, creating bonds with others who share a fascination with the uniqueness of red hair.

However, curiosity can also lead to awkward situations. Some redheads have reported feeling like they are on display—like a prized exhibit at a hair museum. Constant questioning can be exhausting, leading to a desire for privacy. It's crucial to remember that while curiosity can spark meaningful connections, it can also cross boundaries, making individuals feel like their identity is up for public debate, rather than a personal choice.

In the age of social media, the curiosity surrounding red hair has only intensified. Online platforms provide a space for individuals to share their experiences, leading to an outpouring of questions and comments. Hashtags like #RedheadProblems have gained popularity, shining a light on the quirky and often humorous shared experiences of redheads. These digital spaces allow for humor and solidarity, helping navigate the complexities of curiosity in a supportive community—like a virtual hair care support group where everyone understands your plight.

As we explore the spectrum of reactions to red hair, let's celebrate the curiosity that surrounds it. While questions can sometimes feel intrusive, they also serve as a reminder of the beauty of individuality and the power of connection. Red hair may attract attention, but it also opens doors to conversations that enrich our understanding of identity and difference.

Curiosity plays a significant role in shaping how redheads experience their uniqueness. From innocent inquiries to quirky myths, the reactions they receive can lead to both meaningful connections and moments of head-scratching awkwardness. By embracing curiosity while respecting boundaries, we can create a culture that values individuality and celebrates the stories that make each person unique—while ensuring no one feels like a walking hair color chart. As we continue this exploration, we'll delve into the darker side of attention—teasing and bullying—and how these experiences can impact redheads. But fear not, because even in those tales, there's a flicker of humor waiting to shine through.

In the Spotlight

Red hair, with its fiery hues and distinctive flair, has long been a source of fascination—and sometimes, a reason for people to scratch their heads in confusion. While it's a feature that makes its bearers stand out in a crowd (and not just because they might be plotting a dramatic exit), red hair also invites a plethora of stereotypes that can shape how individuals are perceived and treated. In this chapter, we'll explore the common stereotypes associated with redheads, from the amusing to the absurd, delving into their origins and the impact they have on the lives of those who sport this unique hair color.

Stereotypes, by their very nature, simplify complex human experiences, much like trying to explain quantum physics to a cat. They distill individuals into broad categories based on superficial traits, often leading to misunderstandings and misrepresentations. For redheads, the stereotypes can range from the humorous (like being the life of the party, provided the party is in a fiery inferno) to the harmful, often lacking nuance or recognition of individuality. Understanding these stereotypes is crucial, as they influence how redheads interact with the world—and how the world reacts, often with a mix of admiration and bewilderment.

One of the most prevalent stereotypes is the notion of a "fiery temper." The idea that redheads possess an inherent passion and volatility is deeply entrenched in cultural narratives—because who wouldn't want to be known as the human equivalent of a jalapeño? This stereotype paints redheads as unpredictable and quick to anger, which can lead to a significant amount of pressure to conform to this fiery persona. While some may find this association amusing, it can create unrealistic expectations for redheads, compelling them to live up to the stereotype, whether they naturally fit it or not. Sorry, folks, not all redheads are here to throw fireballs!

Another stereotype that has followed redheads throughout history is the association with witchcraft and magic. In various cultures, red hair has been linked to supernatural qualities, with folklore often portraying red-haired individuals as witches or sorceresses. Because who wouldn't want to be mistaken for someone who might turn you into a frog? This stereotype not only romanticizes red hair but also casts a shadow, suggesting that those with this hue might be untrustworthy or mysterious. Imagine showing up to a potluck, and everyone's worried you brought the cursed casserole.

Additionally, there's the quirky and eccentric stereotype that suggests redheads are inherently odd or different. This perception often manifests in media portrayals, where red-haired characters are frequently depicted as the "odd ones out." While celebrating uniqueness is important, reducing individuals to their hair color can be like trying to read a book by only looking at the cover—lots of interesting stuff gets missed.

The perception of redheads as "rare and exotic" is another stereotype worth examining. While it's true that only a small percentage of the global population has naturally red hair, this rarity can create a sense of otherness. It's like being the only unicorn at a horse convention: fascinating at first, but it can get lonely when everyone wants to pet you instead of getting to know you. When people approach redheads with a sense of wonder, it can feel flattering at first, but it may also lead to a disconnect when those individuals realize they are being viewed more as curiosities than as complete people.

The origins of these stereotypes are steeped in history and culture, from ancient texts to modern media. In medieval Europe, red-haired individuals were often associated with devilish traits—because nothing says "I'm a nice person" quite like being compared to the guy in the red jumpsuit. In literature and film, red-haired characters are frequently given traits that align with societal beliefs, reinforcing stereotypes rather than challenging them. These portrayals can create a feedback loop, where stereotypes persist and grow, shaping public perception.

While some redheads might find humor in these stereotypes (and thank goodness for that—laughter is the best hair product), it's essential to recognize that they can have real consequences. Many individuals report feeling the weight of these expectations in their daily lives, affecting their self-esteem and social interactions. The burden of embodying or rebelling against a stereotype can lead to confusion and frustration, leaving redheads navigating a complex landscape of identity. Talk about a hair-raising experience!

In exploring these common stereotypes, we also encounter personal anecdotes from redheads who have lived through these experiences. For some, it's the amused reactions from friends that spark laughter; for others, it's the hurtful jibes that linger long after the words are spoken. These narratives illustrate the varied responses to stereotypes, underscoring the importance of individual experience in understanding the broader implications of these perceptions.

One of the most immediate effects of stereotypes on redheads is the impact on self-image. When individuals are frequently told they have a fiery temperament, it can create an internal conflict. Do they embrace this portrayal, even if it doesn't resonate with their personality? Or do they resist it, feeling the need to prove themselves as calm and collected individuals? This struggle can lead to heightened self-awareness, as redheads navigate their identity in a world that often expects them to fit into predefined boxes. Spoiler alert: no one fits neatly into a box, especially if it's a box labeled "fiery redhead."

In social situations, redheads may find themselves at the center of attention, but not always in a positive light. Friends and acquaintances might joke about their hair color or bring up stereotypes, leading to uncomfortable moments. While some redheads can laugh it off, others may feel singled out or objectified, reducing their identity to mere hair color. The pressure to respond to these comments with grace can be exhausting, turning casual interactions into a performance where redheads feel they must constantly manage perceptions. It's like being in a never-ending episode of "Whose Line Is It Anyway?"—where the points don't matter, but the awkwardness definitely does.

Dating can present unique challenges for redheads, influenced heavily by stereotypes. While many people find red hair alluring and exotic, this attraction can come with strings attached. Some redheads report being seen as "the fiery lover," a stereotype that can complicate romantic relationships. When potential partners view them through the lens of a stereotype, it can hinder authentic connections, leading to superficial interactions where redheads feel they are being valued for their hair rather than their personality. Nothing like getting compliments on your hair while your personality is sitting in the corner, twiddling its thumbs.

Moreover, the workplace is another arena where stereotypes can play a significant role. Redheads may encounter colleagues who approach them with preconceived notions about their temperaments or capabilities. The idea that redheads are quirky can lead to both positive and negative biases, with some employers viewing them as creative thinkers while others may question their professionalism. This duality can create an unpredictable work environment where redheads must constantly negotiate their identities and how they are perceived by others. It's like trying to explain your job to someone while they're distracted by your hair—good luck getting that promotion!

On a more positive note, some redheads leverage stereotypes to their advantage. Embracing the quirky or fiery aspects of their identities can foster camaraderie and connection with others. Humor can become a powerful tool; many redheads learn to use self-deprecating jokes about their hair color to break the ice and deflect attention. This ability to laugh at stereotypes can create a more relaxed atmosphere, allowing for genuine connections to form amidst the playful banter. And hey, if you can't beat them, at least you can make them laugh!

However, the responses to stereotypes can also be more complex. Some redheads may find themselves internalizing negative stereotypes, leading to issues with confidence and self-acceptance. The burden of embodying an ideal can be heavy, especially when it conflicts with one's true nature. For these individuals, social interactions may feel like a minefield, where one misstep could lead to ridicule or judgment. It's like navigating a room full of Lego bricks barefoot—ouch!

Coping mechanisms vary widely among redheads. Some may choose to engage directly with stereotypes, challenging misconceptions head-on. Others might opt for avoidance, steering clear of situations where they feel their hair color will become a topic of discussion. Each response reflects a personal choice shaped by past experiences, highlighting the individuality that exists within the redhead community. And let's be honest, some days it's just easier to stay home and binge-watch cat videos.

Additionally, the rise of social media has transformed how redheads interact with the world. Online platforms provide spaces where red-haired individuals can share their experiences and connect with others who understand the complexities of being a redhead. Hashtags like #RedheadProblems allow for a shared sense of solidarity, offering both humor and support. In these digital spaces, redheads can find community, challenge stereotypes, and embrace their uniqueness in a way that feels empowering. Who knew that a few pixels of hair could foster such camaraderie?

The impact of stereotypes on redheads extends far beyond mere labels; it shapes how they perceive themselves and interact with the world around them. From the challenges of self-image to the complexities of social relationships, these stereotypes can create both barriers and opportunities. By understanding the multifaceted effects of these perceptions, we can foster a more inclusive society that values individuality and recognizes the richness of diverse experiences. So, let's embrace the vibrant spectrum of identities that make up our world, reminding ourselves that our differences are what truly make us unique—especially when those differences involve a fabulous shade of red!

Search for Identity

Navigating the quest for identity can feel like trying to find your way through a labyrinth filled with expectations, stereotypes, and the occasional Minotaur named "Society." You know, the one who insists you wear the right outfit to fit in, even if it makes you feel like you're auditioning for a part in a play you didn't even want to join. The journey usually kicks off in childhood, when we first encounter the delightful—if sometimes bewildering—messages that shape our self-perception. Family, culture, and the ever-watchful gaze of society become the funhouse mirrors reflecting back who we think we should be, warping our image just enough to leave us wondering, "Wait, is that really me?"

From the moment they can say "no," kids start piecing together their sense of self, heavily influenced by family dynamics. Parental expectations, sibling rivalries, and cultural traditions all contribute to the shaping of identities—sort of like a game of "Who Can Put the Most Pressure on You?" For some, this environment fosters confidence and individuality, while for others, it can feel like being wrapped in a blanket of inadequacy, one that's a bit too small and definitely not their color. Imagine being the only person in a room full of fashionable mannequins, feeling out of place in a turtleneck sweater that screams "not my style!" You might find yourself wishing for a fashion intervention or at least a supportive friend to tell you that your neon green socks are a bold choice.

As kids grow, they become increasingly aware of societal norms and expectations, which can lead to a powerful urge to fit in—think of it as an instinct to blend into the wallpaper at a party. Many suppress their unique traits, stifling passions like a budding artist forced to color inside the lines of a very boring coloring book. For example, picture a child with a flair for the dramatic being nudged toward a "more practical" career in accounting—because nothing screams creativity like balancing spreadsheets! Meanwhile, their artistic dreams are tossed aside like last year's fashion.

Self-doubt tends to thrive in environments that prioritize conformity, creating a veritable breeding ground for insecurity. The comparison game begins early, as children start measuring themselves against their peers. This often leads to feelings of inadequacy, with the internal dialogue spiraling into a competition of who has the most exaggerated flaws. It's like a reality show where the only prize is a lifetime of second-guessing and "Am I good enough?" mental gymnastics. You might find yourself wondering if anyone else feels like a misfit in a world full of perfectly polished individuals, or if it's just you, living on the fringes of the "normal" spectrum.

However, the search for identity doesn't exist in a vacuum—thankfully, personal interests and passions can be the magical breadcrumbs leading us out of the labyrinth. Engaging in activities that resonate deeply can provide a sense of belonging and purpose. Whether it's music, sports, or that quirky hobby of collecting rare rubber ducks, these passions can serve as lifelines, reminding us we're more than just walking stereotypes. Imagine finally discovering a group of fellow rubber duck enthusiasts who understand your passion—talk about finding your tribe! Yet, embracing these interests often requires a hefty dose of courage, because nothing says "I'm a rebel!" quite like choosing to love the obscure instead of the mainstream.

As individuals transition into adolescence and adulthood, the search for identity becomes even more pronounced, with societal pressures intensifying like a game of "Can You Top This?" The stakes feel higher, and the question of "Who am I?" echoes in the back of our minds like an annoying pop song stuck on repeat. You might find yourself contemplating existential musings while staring at the ceiling, questioning everything from your career choices to your favorite pizza topping. This journey can be daunting, but it's also a universal experience—after all, we're all just trying to find our way, even if we occasionally trip over our own shoelaces in the process.

Understanding this journey is crucial, as it lays the groundwork for the path toward self-acceptance. Recognizing that the search for identity is complex allows us to approach our experiences with a bit of grace. It encourages exploration without the fear of judgment—because if we can't figure out who we are, at least we can enjoy the ride! It's about taking those awkward dance moves in the middle of a crowded room and realizing that everyone else is too busy worrying about their own moves to notice yours.

The road to self-acceptance is rarely a straight path; instead, it winds through valleys of doubt and peaks of clarity, often detouring through bizarrely specific self-discovery moments, like realizing your obsession with llamas isn't just a phase but a lifelong commitment. Self-awareness becomes the cornerstone of this growth, a vital tool that helps us navigate the labyrinth. It's about recognizing thoughts, feelings, and behaviors in a reflective manner—preferably while holding a cup of tea and wearing fuzzy socks, because self-reflection deserves to be cozy!

However, self-awareness alone won't cut it; we also have to confront those pesky obstacles that hinder our journey. Internal barriers, such as negative self-talk, often sound like a broken record playing the same old hits: "You're not good enough," "You can't sing," and "Put down that rubber duck!" Recognizing the origins of these thoughts is key, as it allows us to challenge and reframe them. Who knew that battling inner critics could be so exhausting? It's like having a mini debate club in your head—where you're the only member and the moderator simultaneously, making it all the more confusing.

External barriers are equally challenging. Social pressures to conform can be like trying to swim upstream in a river of judgmental looks. The fear of rejection often leads us to hide parts of ourselves, stifling our growth like a plant trying to bloom in a dark closet. To overcome these pressures, fostering resilience is crucial—seeking out supportive friendships and communities where individuality is celebrated, like a funky thrift store where everyone can find their unique style. Finding your people can feel like stumbling upon a secret garden filled with the weird and wonderful, where you're free to be as eccentric as you like.

Embracing vulnerability is another vital step on this winding road to self-acceptance. While vulnerability might feel like standing in front of an audience in your pajamas, it's actually a source of strength. Sharing fears, asking for help, or revealing your true self can lead to deeper connections. You might find that when you're brave enough to open up, others follow suit—creating a network of support where everyone can feel a little less alone (and a lot more understood). It's like discovering that your quirks aren't just yours alone; they're part of a larger tapestry that connects us all.

Building a supportive community is essential for nurturing self-acceptance. Surrounding oneself with positive influences—friends, mentors, and fellow rubber duck enthusiasts—reinforces a sense of worthiness. Communities that celebrate diversity create spaces where people can thrive without fear of judgment, allowing everyone to showcase their quirks. It's a bit like hosting a potluck dinner where everyone brings their favorite dish—sometimes messy, often surprising, but always deliciously diverse.

In addition to external support, self-compassion plays a vital role. Learning to treat oneself with kindness, especially when you trip over your own feet (again), is crucial. Self-compassion allows us to appreciate our strengths while acknowledging our imperfections—because let's face it, we're all a bit quirky in our own right. Practicing self-compassion creates a nurturing relationship with ourselves, making it easier to embrace our unique qualities. It's about giving yourself a break when you forget your own birthday or accidentally mix up your appointments—it happens to the best of us!

As we navigate this journey, it's important to remember that it's not linear. There will be moments of progress, followed by setbacks—like a rollercoaster ride where you forgot to check if you were strapped in! Each step, whether forward or backward, contributes to our overall growth, reminding us that the complexity of this journey is what makes it worthwhile. Embracing the messiness of self-discovery can lead to unexpected insights and delightful surprises.

Ultimately, the journey to self-acceptance is about embracing who you are at your core. It's about celebrating the unique combination of experiences, traits, and perspectives that define you—quirks and all! While the road may be fraught with obstacles, it's also filled with opportunities for growth, connection, and joy. As you learn to accept yourself fully, you pave the way for a richer, more authentic existence—one that encourages others to do the same.

Hair Care

Chronicles

Red hair, with its fiery hues and captivating presence, is a striking feature that many envy. Yet, maintaining that vibrant color can sometimes feel like a quest worthy of a heroic tale—think of it as "The Lord of the Locks," but with fewer orcs and more conditioners. From the initial dye job to the daily care that keeps your mane looking fresh, red hair comes with its own set of challenges and delights. In this chapter, we'll explore essential tips and tricks for preserving the brilliance of your red hair, ensuring you shine like the gem you are—or at least like a freshly polished firetruck.

Before we dive into care tips, let's understand what makes red hair unique. Red hair contains a pigment called pheomelanin, which is responsible for its vibrant hues, ranging from strawberry blonde to deep auburn. Unlike other hair colors, red tends to fade more quickly—it's like the party guest who leaves the dance floor too soon. This means that maintaining its vibrancy requires a bit more effort and the right strategies, but don't worry! With the right approach, you can keep your color looking fabulous.

One of the simplest yet most effective ways to keep red hair looking vibrant is to adjust your washing routine. Over-washing can strip natural oils and color, leading to dullness—kind of like showing up to a potluck with nothing but an empty casserole dish. Aim to wash your hair two to three times a week, depending on your hair type. For those with oily hair, consider using dry shampoo to extend the time between washes without sacrificing freshness. Your hair will thank you, and so will your shower curtain.

When you do wash your hair, opt for cool water instead of hot. Hot water can open the hair cuticle, allowing color to escape more easily—like a balloon slowly deflating after a party. A cool rinse helps seal the cuticle, locking in moisture and color. Think of it as giving your hair a refreshing dip in a cool lake instead of a scalding hot tub—much more refreshing! And if you can incorporate a scalp massage while you wash, consider it a mini spa day for your head.

Just like your skin, your hair needs protection from the sun's harmful rays. Ultraviolet (UV) light can fade hair color over time, so consider using hair products that contain UV filters. Hats and scarves can also provide a stylish barrier against the sun, protecting your precious locks while adding flair to your look. Plus, who doesn't love a good accessory? Channel your inner beach diva with a wide-brimmed hat, and you'll be both stylish and sun-savvy.

If you love swimming, be cautious of chlorine. Pools can be a redhead's worst enemy, as chlorine can strip color and cause dryness—like that friend who "borrows" your favorite sweater and returns it three sizes too small. Before swimming, wet your hair with fresh water and apply a leave-in conditioner or protective oil. This will create a barrier and help prevent chlorine from penetrating your hair. And remember, post-swim, rinse your hair thoroughly to remove any chlorine residue. Your hair deserves better than a chemical cocktail!

Keeping red hair hydrated is essential for maintaining its vibrancy. Regular deep conditioning treatments can help restore moisture and shine—think of them as spa days for your hair. Look for products specifically designed for color-treated hair, which often contain nourishing ingredients like argan oil or shea butter. Treat your hair to a deep conditioning mask once a week, and you'll have locks as soft and radiant as a freshly fluffed cloud.

Incorporating a good leave-in conditioner into your daily routine can make a world of difference. These products not only provide moisture but also help protect against environmental stressors. A lightweight leave-in spray can be your hair's best friend, offering hydration and detangling benefits while ensuring your color remains vibrant. After all, who needs a magic wand when you have leave-in conditioner? It's the closest thing to fairy dust we can find in the haircare aisle!

If styling tools are part of your routine, don't forget to use heat protectants. High temperatures can cause damage and contribute to color fading. Apply a heat protectant spray before using blow dryers, straighteners, or curling wands—just think of it as sunscreen for your strands. Your hair deserves the same level of care as your beach-ready skin!

Choosing the right hairstyle can also enhance the beauty of red hair. Loose waves, braids, and updos can showcase the rich tones of your locks. Experiment with styles that allow your hair's natural texture to shine through. And when in doubt, remember that a simple topknot can be both chic and functional, keeping your hair out of your face while still looking fabulous—because let's face it, no one wants hair in their sandwich.

Speaking of fabulousness, I'm thrilled to share that I've recently been invited to be a brand ambassador for the "How to Be a Redhead" brand! I couldn't be prouder to represent a brand that truly understands the needs of redheads everywhere. Their products are specifically designed to enhance and maintain the vibrancy of red hair, making it easier than ever to keep our locks looking radiant. It's like being inducted into a secret society where everyone shares tips on how to keep our fiery hues glowing—pass the hair dye, please!

By following these tips and tricks, you'll be well on your way to maintaining the vibrant red hair that makes you feel confident and unique. Remember, every redhead's journey is different, so don't hesitate to experiment and find what works best for you. And speaking of experiments, don't forget to check out "How to Be a Redhead," which offers a range of products tailored just for us fiery-haired folks.

Come be a brand ambassador with me!
Go to https://sldr.page.link/VfBn

Fashion Flame

With hair that ranges from fiery copper to deep auburn, we're the ones turning heads—sometimes literally, as people do double-takes that rival the best action movie stunts. But being a redhead isn't just about commanding attention; it's a unique fashion journey filled with vibrant choices, unexpected challenges, and, let's face it, a sprinkle of sass.

Let's start with the psychology of color. Red hair isn't just a color; it's a personality trait. It's like wearing a neon sign that says, "Look at me! I'm fabulous!" But with great vibrancy comes great responsibility. You'll often find yourself in a love-hate relationship with your wardrobe as you navigate which colors complement your striking locks and which ones make you look like you just escaped from a fruit salad.

So, what colors work best for redheads? Picture this: you step out in a bright green ensemble that has people gasping in awe. It's like the world is your runway! But then, you decide to try on a yellow dress—oh no! Suddenly, you resemble a walking slice of lemon, and not the cute kind. Think more "citrus horror" than "citrus chic." Who knew that yellow could turn us into the very fruit we enjoy in our morning smoothies?

Now, let's address the stereotypes. Redheads have historically been viewed as either fiery temptresses or feisty troublemakers—thanks, Hollywood! We're often depicted as the quirky best friend or the lovable, hot-headed protagonist. But let's be real: being a redhead means you can pull off just about anything, even if that "anything" is a bizarre choice of oversized plaid pants from the '90s. Hey, they were vintage—until they weren't.

Fashion icons like Lucille Ball and Nicole Kidman have paved the way for redheads to strut their stuff with confidence. I mean, who doesn't want to channel their inner Lucy while rocking a polka-dot dress? And let's not forget those fabulous hair colors that change with the seasons—because who needs a mood ring when you have hair that can signal your emotional state to the entire world? "Oh, you're feeling fiery today? Let's go with a bold crimson!"

Speaking of seasonal changes, let's dive into the world of prints and patterns. Florals? Yes, please!

Stripes? Bring it on! But polka dots? Tread carefully. You might end up looking like a festive ladybug, which, while adorable, may not be the look you're going for when meeting your in-laws for the first time.

Now, onto the struggle of choosing the right wardrobe staples. Every redhead should have some key pieces that celebrate their vibrant hair while making them feel like the superstar they are. Think cozy, oversized sweaters in rich earth tones that contrast beautifully with fiery hair—because who doesn't want to look like a well-dressed autumn leaf?

But here's where it gets tricky. As a redhead, you'll find yourself in the depths of a clothing store, staring at a rack of clothes like you're deciphering ancient hieroglyphics. "Do I dare try that mustard sweater? Am I feeling brave today?" Spoiler alert: you're probably not.

So, how do we embrace our unique style while navigating this colorful labyrinth? The secret is simple: embrace the chaos. Be bold, be sassy, and remember that if you ever wear something that doesn't quite work, you can always blame it on the lighting—or the fact that it was "a mood." After all, every redhead deserves to strut their stuff with unapologetic flair.

Welcome back to the vibrant world of being a redhead! If you thought the first chapter was a wild ride, hold onto your hats (preferably in complementary colors), because we're about to dive deep into the dazzling realm of colors that complement and clash with our fiery manes. It's a veritable fashion rollercoaster, and you'll want to keep your hands and feet inside the ride at all times—especially if you happen to be wearing a shade that clashes with your hair!

Let's kick things off with the colors that harmonize beautifully with red hair. First up: jewel tones. Think deep emerald greens, royal blues, and rich purples. These colors don't just look great; they practically throw a party with your hair! You could walk into a room wearing a deep sapphire dress and watch as jaws drop like it's a magic trick. "How did she do that?" they'll wonder. Spoiler alert: it's all in the color wheel.

Next on the list is earth tones. Browns, beiges, and terracotta shades are like that supportive friend who cheers you on from the sidelines. They enhance your natural beauty without trying to steal the spotlight. And can we talk about how fabulous you'll look in an earthy brown sweater, curled up with a pumpkin spice latte? You'll be the ultimate fall aesthetic, and your Instagram followers will thank you for the seasonal inspiration.

Now, let's address the vibrant reds and pinks. You might think, "More red? Isn't that a bit much?" But hold on a second! When done right, red can be your best friend. Opt for a softer, muted red, or go for a bold fuchsia. Just be cautious about shades that might make you look like you belong in a clown car. You want to embody "fabulous firecracker," not "confused carnival act."

Now, let's play the game of "what to avoid." As redheads, we have a few color landmines lurking in the wardrobe. First on the list: yellow. While sunny hues can brighten a day, wearing yellow as a redhead can sometimes feel like stepping into a bee costume. If you've ever worn yellow and felt like the sun decided to take a vacation just to escape your outfit, you know exactly what I mean. Save those bright yellows for the blondes; they can handle the buzz!

Another tricky contender is orange. You might think, "But I love Halloween!" Trust me, you can still enjoy your pumpkin spice without dressing like one. Orange can clash in ways that are best avoided unless you're intentionally going for that "I just fell into a basket of autumn leaves" look.

Let's also discuss pastel shades. While these can be adorable, they often lack the vibrancy needed to complement your fiery locks. Wearing pastel pink can sometimes make you look like you're auditioning for a role as a cotton candy mascot. And while that could be fun, you might want to save it for a themed party rather than a casual outing.

So, how do you navigate this colorful terrain? It's simple: trial and error. Embrace the power of the fitting room. It's where fashion dreams are made or destroyed—often in a matter of minutes. You'll learn quickly what works for you and what has you running for the exit like you just saw a ghost.

And speaking of ghosts, let's not forget about white. Some redheads can pull off crisp whites with aplomb, but others may find themselves looking like they just stepped off the set of a horror film. "Is she a redhead or a specter?" might be the question on everyone's lips. White can wash you out faster than a bad dye job, so proceed with caution.

As we explore the palette of a redhead's wardrobe, remember: confidence is key. If you feel fabulous in that lime green blouse that makes you look like a human highlighter, own it! Rock that look like you just strutted off the runway. Your hair is a statement; let your clothing be the exclamation point!

In this journey through colors, we also need to talk about accessories. Choosing the right earrings, scarves, or bags can elevate your entire outfit from "meh" to "marvelous." Gold and copper tones tend to work well with red hair, adding a touch of glam without overshadowing your fiery hue. Just remember to avoid any accessories that resemble actual flames—unless you want to start a new trend called "walking bonfire chic."

So there you have it, the colorful world of redhead fashion! With the right colors and a splash of personality, you can transform any outfit into a statement. Embrace the beauty of your vibrant hair, experiment with your wardrobe, and most importantly, have fun!

Welcome to the grand finale, where we pull out all the stops and dive into the art of accessorizing! If you thought your vibrant red hair was the main attraction, just wait until we show you how to take your style to a whole new level. Accessories are the secret sauce that can transform your outfit from "I just threw this on" to "I am a walking masterpiece."

Let's start with the crown jewels—yes, we're talking about jewelry! When you have red hair, choosing the right jewelry can feel like finding a needle in a haystack. You want pieces that complement your fiery mane without clashing like a cat and a dog at a dog show. Gold and copper tones are your best friends here. They enhance the warmth of your hair and add a touch of elegance. Think bold hoop earrings or chunky bracelets that sparkle in the light like you just emerged from a treasure chest.

Now, if you're feeling adventurous, why not experiment with statement pieces? A bold necklace can draw attention to your face and highlight your features. Just make sure it doesn't look like it came from a medieval castle—unless you're going for that "princess trapped in a tower" vibe, in which case, carry on!

Hats are like the cherry on top of your fashion sundae. A chic fedora or a floppy sun hat can add a stylish flair while keeping your hair protected from the sun. Plus, they can help you hide from those days when your hair just refuses to cooperate. "Sorry, I can't come out today—I'm in a committed relationship with my hat."

Scarves are another fabulous accessory that can completely change your look. Wrap one around your neck for a pop of color, or tie it in your hair for a retro vibe. Just remember to avoid anything that resembles a giant orange flag—unless you want to signal that you're ready for a wild adventure!

Let's talk bags. A good handbag can be your trusty sidekick in the quest for style. Opt for bags in complementary colors that enhance your overall look. A deep green or rich burgundy bag can provide that perfect contrast to your red hair. And don't forget about patterns! A fun print can be a great way to express your personality, just be mindful not to clash like two rival bands at a music festival.

Footwear is where things can get really fun. The right shoes can elevate your outfit from casual to catwalk-ready. Think ankle boots, chic flats, or statement heels—just make sure they don't steal the show from your fabulous hair. If you opt for colorful shoes, go for shades that either complement your locks or provide a fun contrast. Just remember, no one wants to look like a walking color wheel!

As you accessorize, keep in mind the balance of your overall look. If you're rocking bold earrings, you might want to tone down other elements to avoid looking like a Christmas tree. It's all about harmony, darling!

Now, let's not forget about makeup. Choosing the right makeup can enhance your red hair beautifully. Warm tones—think peachy blushes, bronzes, and soft golds—can create a stunning effect. And when it comes to lips, deep reds and berry shades can create a knockout combination. Just avoid anything too orange unless you want to look like a bewildered pumpkin at a Halloween party!

Before we wrap this up, let's talk about confidence—because, let's face it, no outfit is complete without it. The most important accessory you can wear is your self-assurance. Strut your stuff like you just won the fashion lottery, and own every look. Confidence can turn a basic outfit into a show-stopping ensemble. When you believe you look good, everyone else will too.

As we conclude this colorful journey through redhead fashion, remember that style is personal. Don't be afraid to experiment, make mistakes, and laugh along the way. Fashion is meant to be fun, and your red hair is a badge of honor that deserves to shine. So go forth, accessorize fearlessly, and let your fabulous self be the center of attention!

And hey, if all else fails, just remember: when in doubt, throw on a statement necklace and a killer pair of shoes. After all, a redhead can make even a potato sack look fabulous—if they wear it with confidence!

Sun-Kissed Science

Welcome to the world of red hair and fair skin, where SPF is a four-letter word and a day at the beach can feel like preparing for an expedition to the sun itself. Let's kick things off with a little science, shall we? Yes, there will be some genetics involved, but don't worry—no lab coats required!

First up, let's talk about the MC1R gene. This little beauty is the reason you've been blessed (or cursed, depending on how you look at it) with your fiery locks and fair complexion. Think of it as the redhead VIP club where only the most exclusive hair colors get in. When you have this gene, you're not just a person; you're a member of a rare breed that gets to experience the world in vivid shades of copper, auburn, and flaming red. It's like walking around with a permanent "look at me!" sign on your head.

Now, here's the kicker: that same gene that makes your hair so stunning also means your skin is as delicate as a soufflé. Fair skin, the kind that can turn a lovely shade of lobster in less than 10 minutes of sun exposure, is linked to your glorious red hair. You're basically walking proof of the age-old adage: "With great power comes great responsibility." But instead of fighting crime, your mission is to avoid sunburn at all costs.

Let's break down the skin types while we're at it. You know that Fitzpatrick scale that sorts us into categories like we're some kind of ice cream flavors? Fair skin is like vanilla—sweet but very prone to melting under the sun. You might find yourself in the "Type I" category, which means you burn faster than you can say "Ouch!" Just one ray of sun, and you'll be sporting a shade that can only be described as "crimson with a hint of regret."

Now, let's tackle some myths. There's this notion floating around that redheads have some secret superpower against sunburn. Spoiler alert: that's just wishful thinking. While you may have a vibrant personality, your skin does not share in that trait. A common misconception is that redheads are impervious to sun damage. This is a classic case of "I saw it on the internet, so it must be true." Newsflash: sunburn does not care what color your hair is; it'll be there faster than you can slather on the sunscreen.

And speaking of sunscreen, let's get into the nitty-gritty of sun protection. You're going to need it—lots of it. Sunscreen should be your new best friend, right up there with chocolate and comfy sweatpants. Aim for an SPF of at least 30, because anything less is like trying to use a Band-Aid on a broken leg. And please, for the love of all things holy, reapply every two hours, especially if you're sweating like a sinner in church or frolicking in the waves. If your idea of a beach day involves any kind of water activity, just consider yourself a walking sunscreen advertisement.

So, now that we've established the relationship between your striking red hair and your porcelain skin, let's embrace it! Sure, you might have to keep a close eye on the UV index, but just think of all the perks. While others are busy blending into the crowd, you're the dazzling peacock strutting through life with hair that can rival the flames of a dragon.

As we journey through this sun-soaked world of redheads and fair skin, remember: knowledge is power, and sunscreen is your shield. Embrace your uniqueness, because in the grand scheme of things, you're not just a redhead; you're a vibrant force of nature—just one that requires a little more SPF and a sun hat that could double as an umbrella.

The sun shines bright, birds chirp, and all seems right with the world—until you remember you're a redhead with fair skin. Suddenly, that sunny picnic in the park transforms into an epic saga of sunburn and questionable choices. Welcome to the thrilling sequel of our sun-soaked adventures!

Let's set the scene: you and your friends decide to head to the beach for a fun day of sunbathing, swimming, and pretending to be mermaids. It's all fun and games until someone forgets the sunscreen, and that someone is usually you. Cue the dramatic music as you step out into the sunlight like a vampire being thrust into daylight. "What fresh hell is this?" you might exclaim as the sun beams down, ready to turn your fair skin into a vibrant shade of "cooked lobster."

Now, let's talk about your relationship with sunscreen. It's complicated, to say the least. You've tried everything—creams, sprays, even the fancy SPF-infused moisturizer that promised you could glow like a goddess. Spoiler alert: you just end up feeling like a greasy frying pan. And let's not forget the dreaded moment when you realize you've applied it unevenly. One arm is a lovely shade of "I just returned from the Caribbean," while the other resembles a ghost trying to sneak out of a horror film.

Ah, but you're determined to have fun! You and your friends set up an elaborate beach tent, complete with snacks, music, and enough towels to create a small fort. As you settle in, a group of sunbathers strolls by, giving you that look—the one that says, "What are you doing under that tent? Are you a vampire?" Yes, yes you are. "Just making sure I don't resemble a tomato by sundown!" you reply with a wink, as they snicker and stroll off to bask in their sun-soaked glory.

Then there's the inevitable beach game: frisbee. Nothing says "I love my fair skin" quite like running around in the sun, trying to catch a flying disc. You're sprinting like an Olympic athlete, but all you can think is, "Why didn't I stay home with a good book?" As you dive for the frisbee, your fair skin glistens with a sheen of sunscreen, and you land in the sand like an awkward dolphin, half-expecting someone to shout, "Cut! That was terrible!"

After a couple of hours of this delightful chaos, you start to feel that familiar tingle on your skin. It's the kind of sensation that says, "Congratulations! You're officially burned." You glance down and realize you've gone from "mildly sun-kissed" to "lobster chic." Your friends are too busy posting perfectly curated Instagram stories of their sun-drenched fun to notice, but you know you've become a cautionary tale in the making.

And what about the joys of trying to cool down after a long day? You head home, completely exhausted, and plop onto your couch like a deflated balloon. You grab a bag of frozen peas (the official redhead remedy) and plop them on your poor, sunburned skin. "Ah, the sweet relief," you sigh. Meanwhile, your friends are still out partying, posting photos that say, "Life's a beach!" while you're contemplating becoming a hermit.

But don't worry! It's not all doom and gloom. You'll find humor in the aftermath. For example, the delightful reactions when people ask what happened to your skin. "Oh, you know, just a little sunbathing!" you'll say, grinning as they recoil in horror at your shade of "well-done." And let's not forget the inevitable question: "Did you use sunscreen?" Yes, Karen, I used sunscreen! In fact, I bathed in it like a sunscreen-loving mermaid!

As you embrace your sunburnt fate, remember this: every redhead has a story of sun exposure that involves a bit of drama, a splash of laughter, and a healthy dose of SPF. Next time you step into the sun, be ready for the wild ride—because life is too short not to laugh at the absurdity of it all. So grab that sunscreen, your trusty hat, and prepare for more adventures in the sun-soaked saga of being fabulously fair-skinned!

Buckle up—it's time for some sun-tastrophes!

Let's begin with that glorious moment when you're finally ready for a day out. You've layered on sunscreen like it's your last chance to protect your fair skin from the elements. You apply it so thickly that you could practically slip-slide your way to the beach. "Who needs a lifeguard?" you joke, "Just call me SPF-40!"

Once you've transformed into a human sunscreen slip 'n slide, it's time for your big adventure. Maybe you've decided on a charming picnic in the park. As you lay out the checkered blanket, you feel like a Pinterest dream come to life. But wait—what's this? The sun is at its peak, and suddenly you're a contestant on a survival reality show. You've got your sunscreen, but have you brought your sun umbrella? Spoiler: you haven't.

So, there you are, trying to find the perfect shady spot under a tree. But it turns out trees are the ultimate trolls of the sun, casting dappled shadows that look nice but offer no real protection. One minute you're lounging, feeling fabulous, and the next, you're developing a freckle tan that could rival a watercolor painting. "Ah, nature," you sigh, "you tricky little imp!"

Now, let's talk about the dreaded moment when you realize you've missed a spot. Yes, that's right! It's the classic redhead dilemma: you've applied sunscreen everywhere—except for that one tiny area on your back that's completely out of reach. The next day, you'll be sporting a sunburn shaped like a target, as if the sun took aim and scored a direct hit. You'll tell your friends you were going for a "minimalist" look, but deep down, you know the truth.

And then there are the awkward encounters with well-meaning strangers. You might be at the beach, looking like a radiant redhead goddess, when someone feels the need to comment, "You really should put on some sunscreen!" You want to respond with, "Thanks, Captain Obvious! But don't worry, I'm just auditioning for the role of 'Human Lobster' in my next big movie!" Instead, you smile politely while silently plotting your revenge with an imaginary bucket of sunscreen.

Let's not forget the post-sun exposure beauty routine. You know, the one that involves slathering on aloe vera like you're frosting a cake? You go from "fun in the sun" to "a walking aloe plant" in no time. And of course, you can't escape the stares when you go out in public, smelling like a tropical oasis while trying to convince people it's a trendy new fragrance. "No, really! It's called 'Sunburn Bliss!'"

Then there are those times when you think, "Maybe I can handle just a little sun without the SPF." Ah, the naiveté! You venture out for a casual stroll, convinced your red hair will somehow protect you. Fast forward a few hours: you're a walking advertisement for why SPF is non-negotiable. Your skin is now more reminiscent of a tomato than a sun-kissed glow, and you're left wondering how you'll explain this to your future self in the mirror. "Well, past me, we're definitely not going to the beach again without a full-body suit of sunscreen!"

As the sun begins to set, you find yourself covered in aloe, feeling a mix of triumph and regret. You survived another sun-soaked day, and it's time to reflect. You sit down with a cold drink (preferably something fruity and tropical) and laugh about the day's adventures, noting how you've become a pro at turning every sun disaster into a comedy routine. "I should really get a stand-up gig!" you chuckle.

In the end, whether you're rocking the "lobster chic" look or embracing your aloe-infused state, remember that sun exposure is just part of the redhead experience. Life's too short to take it too seriously! So, as you embark on your next outdoor adventure, don't forget your sunscreen, your sense of humor, and the unwavering belief that you can totally rock this fair-skinned life—one SPF disaster at a time!

Now that you're fully armed with laughter and knowledge about sun exposure, get ready for your next adventure! Whether it's lounging by the pool, hiking under the blazing sun, or simply trying to enjoy a sunny day, you're ready to tackle it all—with a hefty side of sunscreen, of course!

The Ginger Dating Game

Ah, the dating pool! It's a lot like a kiddie pool—filled with questionable choices, splashes of chaos, and the occasional floatie that just won't sink. But for redheads, it's a whole different swimming experience. You see, when you have hair that ranges from fiery copper to deep auburn, stepping into the dating scene is like cannonballing into a pool of jellybeans: everyone notices, and some may even want a taste!

Let's face it, being a redhead means you're immediately a walking conversation starter. Picture this: you're at a bar, sipping your drink, and across the room, you spot a potential date. You make eye contact, and boom! The intrigue is real. But just as you're about to flash your best smile, you can practically hear the inner dialogue of that potential suitor: "Wow, she's gorgeous! I wonder if she's as fiery as her hair—or if it's just a marketing ploy."

Now, being a redhead isn't just about the hair color; it's a full-blown persona. The stereotypes kick in faster than you can say "Ginger Snap." You're either seen as a spicy seductress or a quirky, fun-loving sidekick—think Lucille Ball meets a spicy pepper. It's a delicate balancing act, like walking a tightrope made of hair dye and expectation.

Let's dive into the world of attention. If you thought you were going to quietly blend into the background on a date, think again! You'll likely find yourself the center of attention, and not always for the reasons you want. Sure, there are those sweet compliments like, "Your hair is stunning!" and "I've always wanted to date a redhead!" But then there are the not-so-subtle comments that can make you cringe, like, "Do you dye it, or is it natural? Because I heard redheads are like unicorns—very rare!" Newsflash: if I had a nickel for every time I heard that, I could buy a unicorn.

Now, let's talk about the mixed reactions redheads get. You'll encounter people who act like they've just spotted a rare Pokemon. There's excitement, curiosity, and maybe a little bit of fear—like they might get burned just by being near your fiery locks. You can almost see their minds racing, "Should I catch it or run away?" Spoiler alert: some will try to catch you with cheesy pick-up lines that are so bad, they might as well come with a side of cringey emojis.

"Are you from Tennessee? Because you're the only ten I see!" Ah yes, nothing like a classic line that makes you want to roll your eyes and check your escape routes.

But let's not ignore the dark side of this attention. With great vibrancy comes great responsibility—or at least a few awkward encounters. Picture this: you're on a date, and as you're sharing a funny story about your most embarrassing moment, you notice the waiter staring at you like you just performed a magic trick. You pause, wondering if you've inadvertently revealed a hidden talent. Nope, just your hair reflecting the light like a disco ball, causing the entire restaurant to question their life choices.

Then there's the phenomenon of hair envy. Have you ever noticed how some people can't help but touch your hair? One minute, you're enjoying a charming dinner conversation, and the next, someone's reaching out like they're trying to pet a rare breed of dog. "Is it soft?" they ask, as if you might respond, "Well, let me put it this way: I shampooed it with unicorn tears today."

As if that weren't enough, redheads often find themselves fielding questions about their fiery locks that border on the absurd. "What's it like being a redhead?" they ask, as if you're secretly a member of a mystical society. "Do you really have a temper?" Spoiler alert: the answer is yes, but only when you forget to bring a snack on a long date. Hangry redheads are not to be trifled with!

As we plunge deeper into the dating pool, remember this: the attention you receive can be both a blessing and a curse. You might feel like a celebrity one moment and a circus act the next. Embrace the chaos, revel in the quirkiness, and don't forget to laugh it off. After all, being a redhead means you're already a vibrant splash in a sea of monotony. So go forth, fellow redhead, and own that spotlight like it's your runway!

Now that we've established that our hair is basically a built-in spotlight, let's talk about how to dress to keep that spotlight shining brightly—and without causing a fashion meltdown. Because let's face it, redheads can be as colorful in our wardrobes as we are in our hair, and we need to navigate those choices with the finesse of a seasoned tightrope walker.

First things first: the outfit choice is crucial. Think of it as your first impression's grand entrance. You want to strike that perfect balance between eye-catching and "please don't ask me to wear a clown costume." Let's be honest, no one wants to look like they accidentally wandered into a carnival while on their way to a romantic dinner.

One of the golden rules for redheads is to embrace jewel tones. Deep emerald greens, rich blues, and bold purples? Yes, please! These colors complement your fiery mane like a fine wine with a gourmet meal. You could waltz into a date in a deep sapphire dress, and suddenly it feels like the universe has aligned to make you the star of a rom-com. "Wow, you look amazing!" your date will exclaim, and you'll respond with a casual, "Oh, this old thing? I just threw it on." Little do they know, you spent an hour curating the perfect ensemble.

Now, let's talk about the colors to avoid. Remember our good friend, yellow? While it might look sunny and cheerful in theory, wearing it as a redhead can make you resemble a walking banana split—minus the delicious ice cream. So unless you're planning to be a dessert-themed date, steer clear. And please, let's have a collective agreement to avoid orange. We love Halloween as much as the next person, but we don't want to turn into a giant pumpkin on our date!

Patterns can also be a double-edged sword. Florals are your friends—think vibrant blooms that echo your vivaciousness—but tread carefully with stripes. Vertical stripes can be flattering, but horizontal ones? Let's just say you might end up looking like a human candy cane, and not in a cute holiday way. And polka dots? Approach with caution. They can either make you look whimsical or like you're auditioning for a role as a cartoon character.

Next, let's discuss the importance of fit. We all know that the right fit can make or break an outfit.

You want to accentuate your best features while feeling comfortable enough to eat that second slice of pizza without feeling like a stuffed turkey. Tailored pieces that hug in the right places will boost your confidence and keep your date's eyes focused on you, not the awkward bulge from last night's takeout.

And here's a little secret: accessories can elevate your look from "meh" to "marvelous" in seconds. A statement necklace can draw attention to your lovely face (and fabulous hair, of course) while a stylish handbag can add a pop of personality. Just remember not to go overboard—if your jewelry starts to jingle louder than your laughter, it might be time to tone it down.

Footwear is where things can get interesting. Whether you opt for chic flats or sky-high heels, just ensure they align with the vibe of your date. A hike in stilettos is a bold choice, but unless you want to end up with sore feet and a few questionable photos, maybe stick to something that says, "I can walk, dance, and still look fabulous."

Now let's touch on makeup. As a redhead, your makeup can either enhance your look or turn you into a circus act. Warm tones work wonders—think peach blush and soft gold eyeshadow. And when it comes to lips, deep reds can be your best friend. Just avoid anything too bright or neon unless you want to give off the vibe that you're ready to hit the disco instead of that intimate café.

But what about those days when you're just not feeling it? Fear not! There's always the trusty "I woke up like this" look. A cute oversized sweater paired with skinny jeans can exude effortless chic while still making a statement. Throw in a messy bun and a swipe of lip balm, and suddenly you're the coolest redhead in the room—perfect for a casual coffee date or brunch where the most important question is "Mimosas or Bloody Marys?"

Now, let's not forget the beauty of confidence. The most stunning outfit can fall flat if you're not rocking it with self-assurance. So, whether you're strutting in your favorite dress or rocking jeans and a tee, remember: confidence is the ultimate accessory. If you believe you look good, your date will pick up on that energy faster than you can say "fabulous."

Oh, the pick-up lines! As a redhead, you're often met with some creative attempts at flirtation. "Do you have a map? Because I just got lost in your hair!" is a classic, but you can only hear that so many times before you start wondering if they actually believe you're a sentient GPS device. And then there's the inevitable, "What color is your hair?" as if you're not rocking the world's most vibrant shade. Spoiler alert: it's red. It's always red.

Then there are the charming folks who, upon spotting you, feel compelled to inform you of their redhead factoid knowledge. "Did you know redheads have more fun?" they exclaim, as if they've just discovered the secret to eternal happiness. Sure, we might have a blast, but it's usually while trying to figure out how to get that pesky hair dye out of the bathtub. So, thanks for the fun fact, but we're living the struggle over here!

Let's not forget those awkward moments when someone tries to compliment you—only for it to go hilariously wrong. Picture this: you're at a romantic dinner, feeling fabulous in your jewel-toned ensemble, and your date leans in, smiles, and says, "You know, redheads are just so… fiery." Cue the eye-roll that could probably power a small village. "Really? Did you think I was a cute little ember? Because I assure you, I'm more of a blazing inferno!"

Then there's the experience of meeting the parents. Imagine walking into their home, hair ablaze, and they look at you like you're an exotic species that just landed from another planet. "So, what's the deal with your hair?" they ask, completely ignoring your date's actual personality. Suddenly, you're on display like a rare butterfly in a glass case, and all you want to do is blend in with the wallpaper. "Uh, yes, my hair is red. I came here to meet you, not to audition for a circus act!"

And speaking of family gatherings, can we talk about the dreaded "so when are you two getting married?" question? It's like a rite of passage for any couple, but for redheads, it's usually accompanied by a bewildered look from relatives who can't figure out why you're dating someone without the same hair color. "But what about the red-haired babies?" they gasp, clutching their pearls as if your hair color is the only factor in determining your future children's hair.

Let's not overlook the unexpected perks of dating as a redhead, though! First dates often come with bonus entertainment: people's reactions. When you walk into a bar or restaurant, heads will turn, jaws will drop, and suddenly it's like you're the main attraction at a side show. "Is that hair real?" they'll whisper, half-expecting to see a unicorn prancing beside you. You can't help but feel like a celebrity—albeit one who's just trying to enjoy a quiet evening out.

Now, if there's one thing every redhead can agree on, it's the sheer joy of dating someone who truly appreciates your hair. When you finally find that special someone who not only admires your fiery locks but also understands the daily struggle of color-treated hair, it feels like a small victory. "Wow, your hair is so vibrant!" they'll say, and you'll respond with, "Thanks! It only took an entire life of trial and error!"

As you navigate the dating scene, remember that the most important part of this journey is to have fun. Embrace the chaos, the laughter, and the absurdity of it all. Sure, there will be awkward moments and cringe-worthy pick-up lines, but those experiences are what make the dating world so wonderfully unpredictable.

So, whether you're rolling your eyes at yet another fiery compliment or basking in the glory of being the star of your own romantic comedy, embrace the redhead experience with flair. After all, it's not just about finding love; it's about making unforgettable memories, one fabulous date at a time.

Redhead Family Tree

Imagine a family gathering where the first thing you notice is a vivid explosion of hair colors that could rival a paint store's display. Welcome to the world of redhead families, where each member seems to compete for the title of "Most Vibrant Hair." It's like Thanksgiving dinner, but instead of turkey, you're served a platter of fiery locks and spirited debates.

The moment you step into the room, someone inevitably shouts, "Did you dye your hair?" It's a classic opener that never gets old. This leads to a flurry of explanations about the complex genetics behind red hair—because let's face it, there's always that one relative who's an amateur geneticist. "It's all about the MC1R gene," they'll announce proudly, before anyone can ask them to pass the mashed potatoes. And just when you thought you were here to eat, now you're in a seminar on hair color genetics.

As everyone settles in, the real fun begins: the stories. "You know, your great-aunt Ethel had hair so red it glowed in the dark!" This is usually followed by a collective gasp of admiration and a few whispered "what happened to her?" glances. Ethel's legendary hair is a topic of endless fascination, as if she's some kind of mythical creature, possibly the original 'Redhead of the family. There's always one person who claims they have the same shade, as if by association, they too can channel Ethel's supernatural glow.

And let's not ignore the competitive spirit that runs through redheaded families like a strong cup of Irish coffee. At least once during the evening, someone will propose a game: "Who's the most vibrant?" This leads to a fashion show of sorts, with everyone trying to outdo each other. Uncle Dave struts around, flaunting his bright orange hair like a peacock, while Aunt Linda swishes her auburn locks like she's in a shampoo commercial. The kids? They're just trying to figure out how to add glitter to their hair without getting caught by the parents.

In the midst of this chaos, someone will pull out their phone and scroll through the "Redhead Memes" Facebook group. "Oh look!" they'll announce, "Someone shared a meme about being a redhead in a family of blondes!" Cue the uproarious laughter, because every redhead knows that feeling of being the odd one out, even if you're surrounded by a crowd of your own kind.

Then comes the inevitable topic of hair care routines. "You have to use special shampoo!" someone insists, as if they're revealing the secret to eternal youth. "And don't forget the conditioner! Your hair needs moisture, especially with how fiery it is!" By the end of the night, you'll have a new beauty regimen that involves ingredients you can't even pronounce, all while secretly wondering if you'll ever actually follow through.

As the evening progresses, you'll find yourself reminiscing about your own hair adventures. "Remember when you thought you could pull off that bright pink streak?" someone chimes in. Laughter ensues, along with a few "please don't remind me" groans. Each story shared only adds to the ever-growing lore of the family, turning your shared hair color into a tapestry of mishaps and triumphs.

By the time dessert rolls around, you've collectively crafted a family narrative that's as colorful as the hair on your heads. You may be a bunch of redheads, but you're also a cast of characters that could fill a sitcom: the quirky aunt, the competitive uncle, and the kids who just want to make it through the night without a hair dye incident. And just like that, in a whirlwind of laughter and wild hair, you realize that being part of this redhead family is not just about the hair color—it's about the memories, the laughter, and the undeniable bond that ties you all together.

Redheads are often associated with a fiery temperament. It's like we were all born with a built-in heatwave. Picture this: Aunt Mary bursts into the room, hair aflame, announcing that she's just returned from a heated debate at the local book club. "They dared to say 'Harry Potter' isn't a classic!" she fumes, her hair practically vibrating with indignation. We all nod knowingly, because we've seen the redhead fury unleashed over far less.

Meanwhile, the kids sit on the sidelines, wide-eyed and taking mental notes. "Is it a family trait to get riled up over fictional wizards?" they might wonder. Spoiler alert: yes. Welcome to the family, kiddos; prepare for some lively dinner conversations.

Next up on our tour of quirks is the infamous redhead sensitivity. You know what I mean—sunburns that happen at the mere suggestion of sunlight. At family gatherings, the redhead kids come armed with SPF 5000, looking like tiny astronauts preparing for a space mission rather than a picnic. "Remember, only the sunscreen will protect you!" parents chant like a mantra, while the fair-skinned kids nod solemnly, secretly hoping to avoid the dreaded lobster look.

And then there are the hair-related superstitions. Redheads, we all know, are supposed to bring good luck—or bad luck, depending on who you ask. One family member might swear that every time they cut their hair, something fabulous happens, like finding a $20 bill or being asked out on a date. Meanwhile, another cousin is convinced that the last time they dyed their hair, it coincided with their cat losing its collar. Clearly, it's a complicated web of omens, and no one is quite sure how it works.

Of course, the quirks extend to fashion choices, too. Redheads often feel a deep, spiritual connection to bold colors. If it's bright, it's in. But heaven help anyone who tries to dress a redhead in beige. "What am I? A potato?" we might exclaim, clutching our vibrant garments like a shield against the mundane. Family members often end up dressed like walking highlighters, and there's always one daring soul who insists they can pull off plaid. Spoiler: they can't.

As we gather around the dinner table, discussions often veer toward the genetic lottery. "I got the curly hair from Grandma, and the fiery temper from you, Dad," one cousin will joke, causing an uproar of laughter. "And I got the good looks," another will chime in, flipping their hair dramatically. These exchanges happen every time, but no one gets tired of the banter. Because with each quirk, each shared laugh, you can feel the family bond tightening, knitting you all together into a tapestry of red-haired hilarity.

Then there are the "Redhead Memes" that circulate within the family group chat. One day, someone shares a meme about the struggles of redhead parenting: "When your kid's hair gets brighter than yours, and you're not sure whether to celebrate or call a hairdresser." Cue the endless comments and GIFs, as everyone pitches in with their own stories about hair disasters or triumphs. "Remember when Timmy tried to dye his hair purple and ended up looking like a grape?" someone will inevitably remind everyone, triggering a wave of laughter and a few sympathetic head shakes.

As dessert rolls around, the conversations take a reflective turn. Amidst the jokes and shared quirks, it's clear that every redhead in the room carries the legacy of their predecessors. Whether it's Ethel's legendary hair or Aunt Mary's fiery debates, these traits become stories passed down through generations, each infused with a bit of humor and a whole lot of love.

As we gather for the annual family reunion—an event that can only be described as a vibrant circus of redheads—one thing becomes crystal clear: our family dynamics are as colorful and unpredictable as our hair. The air buzzes with laughter, teasing, and the occasional burst of fiery tempers. It's a reminder that being part of this clan is like being on an unending rollercoaster—thrilling, chaotic, and a little dizzying.

Let's talk about the family stories that float around like confetti at a party. Every gathering brings forth the legendary tales of our ancestors. There's the infamous story of Great Uncle Jerry, who attempted to dye his hair green for St. Patrick's Day and ended up with a permanent "Shrek" look that haunted him for years. "It was supposed to be festive!" he insists, while the rest of us are doubled over in laughter. These stories are more than just entertainment; they're the fabric of our family history, a shared legacy of eccentricity and laughter.

The conversation often veers into the territory of "who inherited what." You might hear someone shout, "I got my fiery temper from Grandma, but I definitely got my patience from the mailman!" Each jab is met with playful eye rolls and good-natured rebuttals. The family dynamics here are a well-oiled machine of love, teasing, and undeniable support. Every jibe is a reminder that no matter how quirky our traits, we stand united in our redheaded heritage.

And then there's the inevitable "Redhead Traits Showdown," where each family member tries to outdo the others with their quirkiest inherited trait. "I can't tan! I just burn and then turn back into a ghost!" one cousin exclaims, and everyone nods knowingly. "Well, I have the emotional range of a soap opera character!" another counters, dramatically clutching their chest. The laughter swells as we recount the ridiculousness of it all, embracing the chaos that comes with being a redhead.

One evening, as the sun sets and the golden light casts a warm glow over our gathering, someone brings up a meme from the "Redhead Memes" group. It's a hilarious cartoon about how redheads get recognized in a crowd—instantly—and how we often have to navigate the challenges that come with being so visually striking. "Every time I walk into a room, I feel like a celebrity," one family member quips. "It's exhausting!"

But amidst the laughter, there's a moment of reflection. We begin to share stories of the strength and resilience that run through our family. It's not just about the fiery tempers or the vibrant hair; it's about the legacy of redheads who have faced challenges with tenacity and humor.

From Grandma who fought her way through a world that often dismissed her, to Uncle Bob, who turned his struggles into comedy, our family has shown that our quirks make us stronger. We embrace our differences, and every laugh shared is a testament to our bond.

As the night winds down and the fire crackles, we gather for one last toast. "To the redheads!" someone shouts, raising their glass high. "May our hair be fiery, our tempers fierce, and our love for each other as vibrant as our manes!" The cheers erupt around the circle, a cacophony of joy and unity.

In the end, being part of this red-haired family isn't just about hair color or inherited traits. It's about the moments we share, the laughter that rings through the air, and the love that binds us all together. Each quirky story, each inherited quirk, and every fiery personality trait weaves into a beautiful tapestry of who we are.

As the last of the night's light fades and the stars twinkle overhead, one thing remains certain: our family, like our hair, is a unique blend of wild colors and crazy stories, and we wouldn't have it any other way.

104

Our Community

What really ties us redheads together? It's not just the fiery locks that sparkle in sunlight or the inevitable sunburn we all experience at the beach—no, it's the shared experiences that create our very own ginger bond. You see, we redheads have an unspoken code, a camaraderie that comes from navigating life with hair that could stop traffic. We understand each other in a way that others simply can't. "Oh, your hair gets frizzy in the humidity too? Welcome to the club!"

Let's talk about the infamous redhead experiences that bring us together. For starters, there's the eternal quest for the right hair products. As if finding a shampoo that doesn't leave us looking like a frizzy poodle wasn't challenging enough, we also have to dodge the minefield of hair dye mishaps. "This shade is 'Cinnamon Spice,'" they say. "It'll look great!" And then you emerge from the salon looking more like a Christmas ornament than the sultry spice you envisioned. Cue the sympathetic gasps from fellow redheads: "I know exactly how you feel; I once ended up with 'Burnt Toast' instead of 'Cherry Bomb.'"

Then there's the inevitable sunburn. Ah, the sun: that giant flaming ball of light that thinks it's hilarious to roast us like marshmallows. We step outside, and suddenly it's like the sun says, "Oh, look! A redhead! Let's see how quickly we can turn her into a lobster!" You know it's bad when you have to slather on aloe vera and wear a wide-brimmed hat that makes you look like you're auditioning for a role in a bad Western. "I'm just here to find my lost cattle!" you shout, while the world stares at your neon-red nose.

But what truly unites us is the quirky support system we've developed over the years. You see, redheads have this magical ability to spot each other from a mile away—especially in a crowded room filled with not-so-golden locks. It's like a secret radar that goes off. "Redhead alert! Three o'clock!" Suddenly, we're bonding over shared sunscreen brands and the eternal question: "Do you also carry around a personal fan?" Because, let's be honest, we're practically heat-sensitive walking thermometers.

And then there's the online community. Social media has given us the chance to unite like never before. Ever heard of the "Redhead Memes" group on Facebook? It's like a comedy club where every post is a love letter to our uniqueness. One member recently shared a hilarious story about her grandmother, who claimed that all redheads were descended from the fiery spirits of ancient warriors. "I mean, that explains my need to conquer snack time," she joked, and suddenly we all felt a little more validated in our quest for chips at midnight.

So, there we are, a motley crew of red-haired warriors, united by our shared experiences and the undeniable bond of being fabulously unique. From the hair mishaps to the sunburn stories, we form a community that can laugh, cry, and share advice on how to best handle that one cousin who insists that redheads have a special "fiery curse." Spoiler: the only curse we have is a penchant for feeling awkward in photos when everyone else is sporting sleek, glossy locks.

If there's one thing redheads know how to do, it's throw a party. And when it comes to gatherings, we're all about making it a fiery affair. Whether it's a local meet-up, a global festival, or a spontaneous get-together over a pitcher of sangria, redheads know how to unite and celebrate our unique flair.

Let's kick things off with the legendary Redhead Day, held annually in the picturesque city of Breda in the Netherlands. Imagine a sea of redheads taking over the streets—an eye-popping spectacle that can only be described as a ginger tsunami.

There are contests for the brightest hair, games that involve tug-of-war (because nothing says "team spirit" like a good old-fashioned showdown), and of course, plenty of photo ops that make you feel like you're in a scene from a blockbuster movie. "Forget the Avengers; the real heroes have fiery hair!"

But the fun doesn't stop there. Oh no, my friends! Picture this: an international gathering where redheads from all over the world come together, each with their own stories, quirks, and shades of red. You've got the copper-haired beauties mingling with the auburn goddesses, each of us eyeing each other's locks with a mix of admiration and jealousy. "How do you get yours to shine like that?" you ask, and suddenly it's a hair product swap meet. "This conditioner will change your life!" It's like an infomercial, but with more laughter and fewer awkward pauses.

Then there's the phenomenon of "Redhead Meet-ups," where local groups organize outings that can include anything from picnics to bar crawls. You walk into a bar and instantly know it's a redhead event because there's a special energy in the air. There's a certain sparkle that can only come from a gathering of people who understand the struggle of frizzy hair on humid days. And, of course, we're all well-versed in the art of "redhead spotting." "Look! A fellow fiery friend!" you exclaim, pointing as if you've spotted a rare species in the wild.

Now, let's talk about the games we play. Have you ever tried a redhead-themed trivia night? It's like a regular trivia night, but the questions are all about our unique experiences. "What shade of red is known to cause immediate compliments?" Spoiler alert: it's "Anything But Dull." The stakes are high, and the laughter is even higher as we reminisce about the ridiculous comments we've received over the years. "No, I didn't dye it; I was born this way!" becomes the unofficial motto of the night.

And then there are the global festivals dedicated to all things redhead. Picture a carnival atmosphere, complete with food trucks serving up the most delicious snacks, local bands belting out tunes, and contests to see who can do the best imitation of a ginger-haired cartoon character. You'll find redhead face painting (because why not?), talent shows, and workshops on how to embrace your fiery personality. "How to Be Fiery and Fabulous 101" becomes a must-attend class, and by the end, we all walk away with more confidence than we started with.

Of course, no redhead gathering would be complete without the obligatory photo booth. Who doesn't love posing with oversized props like flaming torches or signs that say "Redheads Unite!"? We strike our best poses, and as the flash goes off, you can almost hear the collective roar of laughter. "Do I look like a fire-breathing dragon yet?" you ask, while your friends respond with enthusiastic nods.

But let's not forget the stories that come out of these gatherings. You'll hear tales of redheads who've faced the trials and tribulations of being unique, from the struggles of finding hair products that work to the hilarity of family gatherings where every relative wants to talk about their "fiery heritage." "Oh, you're a redhead? Your grandmother must have been a witch!" someone exclaims, and suddenly everyone is sharing their own family myths and legends.

f there's one thing we've learned, it's that being a redhead comes with its own set of rules—like an exclusive club with a secret handshake (which, let's be real, usually involves tossing your hair dramatically). You've got your redhead survival kit down to a science: SPF 50 for those sunny days, a trusty hat for the wild wind, and, of course, a go-to stylist who knows the art of keeping those fiery locks vibrant.

And how about those classic sayings that have become our unofficial motto? "Redheads have more fun" is an absolute truth. We embrace life with a passion that's hard to match, whether we're dancing like no one's watching or launching into animated debates about which shades of red are the most fabulous. "Oh, you think auburn is the best? Please! It's all about the copper!" This is not just a preference; it's a way of life!

Let's not forget the shared experiences that bind us. Who hasn't had that moment of solidarity when you meet another redhead in the wild? The double-take, the grin, and the immediate bond formed over the shared trials of being a walking attention magnet. From unsolicited questions about our hair care routines to the classic, "Do you have a temper?" we've all been there. Those moments are like a rite of passage, and they create an unspoken understanding that's hard to break.

Now, as we look ahead, it's essential to think about the next generation of redheads. Will they have the same fiery spirit? Absolutely! With gatherings and events continuing to thrive, the legacy of redhead camaraderie is in safe hands. Think of all the little gingers running around, unaware of the incredible community that awaits them. They'll grow up hearing tales of Redhead Day and stories of their ancestors who dared to stand out in a crowd. "Did you know Grandma used to be a total diva at the redhead rallies?" will be a favorite anecdote passed down, filled with laughter and pride.

As technology advances, so does our ability to connect. Online communities are flourishing, and platforms like the "Redhead Memes" Facebook group serve as digital watering holes for sharing experiences, humor, and, of course, memes that only we would understand. The inside jokes about sunburns, fiery tempers, and shampoo disasters become a delightful bonding tool. "When the sun is out, it's a redhead's plight," one meme might say, perfectly encapsulating our struggles with a dash of humor. These connections remind us that even in our virtual world, the spirit of redheaded unity shines brightly.

And let's not forget the importance of supporting each other, whether it's through humor, shared experiences, or simply being there when one of us needs a boost. When one redhead shines, we all shine a little brighter. It's the ultimate pep rally, where we cheer each other on and celebrate our individual quirks. "You dyed your hair flamingo pink? You go, girl!" becomes our battle cry as we embrace each other's journeys.

A "POP" of Red

Throughout history, redheads have been portrayed in a dazzling array of roles, from mystical figures to fierce warriors. If you've ever found yourself daydreaming about how your fiery locks could have fit into ancient tales, this chapter is for you! Let's take a lighthearted stroll through the annals of history and literature, exploring how redheads have made their mark—sometimes in ways that make us chuckle, and other times in ways that leave us raising our eyebrows.

First stop: the world of mythology. Many ancient cultures have recognized the fiery allure of red hair, often associating it with divinity or danger. Take the legendary Norse god Loki, the trickster whose hair was often depicted as a vibrant red. While he wasn't exactly a paragon of virtue—more of a "let's cause some mischief and see what happens" kind of guy—he certainly embodied that wild, unpredictable energy we often associate with redheads. Can you imagine him showing up to a party? "Hey, everyone! Let's turn this feast into a giant game of charades! Winner gets to steal the spotlight!"

In Celtic mythology, red hair is frequently linked to the otherworldly and the passionate. Take the tale of the legendary warrior queen Boudica. With her wild, red mane and fierce spirit, she led her people in revolt against the Romans. Picture this: Boudica on a battlefield, hair flowing like a dramatic cape, rallying her troops with a rousing speech that probably went something like, "Let's show them what a redhead can do! Spoiler: it's not just a great hairstyle!"

Moving on to literature, we find redheads featured prominently in the works of Shakespeare. Who could forget the fiery-haired character of Lady Macbeth? She's the ultimate "power behind the throne" figure, with ambition that burns hotter than her hair color. And let's be real: when she calls upon the spirits to "unsex" her, you can practically hear the audience collectively gasping, "Whoa, she means business!" It's almost as if red hair in literature comes with a sign that says, "Caution: fiery ambition ahead!"

Fast forward to the Victorian era, where redheads were often depicted as either passionate heroines or the mysterious temptresses who led unsuspecting gentlemen into a world of scandal. Think of *Jane Eyre*'s fiery-haired protagonist—her passionate nature and independence make her the ultimate literary heroine. Yet, she navigates a world that can be as stifling as a corset. "How dare you suppress my fiery spirit?" she might exclaim, tossing her head back with flair. Meanwhile, some contemporary adaptations have turned this spirited character into a somewhat subdued version, perhaps missing the mark on how vibrant and rebellious redheads can truly be.

Then there's the classic children's literature featuring our fiery-haired friends. Anne of Green Gables is perhaps the most iconic redhead in literary history. With her wild imagination and penchant for disaster, Anne Shirley is a breath of fresh air. One can almost hear her lamenting, "Why can't I just be a normal girl with normal hair?" To which the universe responds, "Because you're too fabulous for that!" Anne's adventures serve as a delightful reminder that embracing one's uniqueness can lead to some of life's greatest joys.

But not all depictions have been rosy. Throughout history, redheads have also been associated with witchcraft and other nefarious activities. In medieval Europe, the "red-haired witch" stereotype flourished, leading to accusations and trials that left many innocent redheads in hot water (not the kind they prefer!). Picture a village where the redheaded woman is accused of witchcraft because her hair "sparkles in the sunlight"—talk about an unfair advantage! It's a reminder that while redheads might turn heads for their beauty, it's not always been in a good way.

As we explore these historical and literary representations, it's clear that redheads have often been cast as the misfits, the outsiders, and the wild spirits. But what does this say about our identity today? These stories, while often exaggerated, have woven a rich tapestry of who we are, reflecting both the struggles and the triumphs of those fiery souls who came before us.

In modern media, we find a resurgence of redheaded characters that reflect a broader spectrum of personalities. No longer confined to the "fiery" archetype, redheads are now portrayed in a multitude of ways, from quirky nerds to powerful leaders. This evolution in representation allows contemporary redheads to feel more seen and celebrated, rather than pigeonholed into one-dimensional roles.

If Hollywood had a dollar for every time a redhead was cast as the "spunky troublemaker" or "mischievous firebrand," we'd all be sipping lattes on our private islands by now. Seriously, it's like casting directors received a memo that said, "If the character has red hair, make sure they have an attitude to match!" Is there an unwritten rule that redheads must also have a fiery personality? Apparently, it's in the hair dye.

Take the classic trope of the "fiery temptress." We've all seen her: sultry red locks cascading down her shoulders as she seduces the hero with a wink and a promise of adventure. She's the one who makes you question your life choices while simultaneously hoping she's not plotting something diabolical. While we appreciate the flair, can we also get a redhead who's just… chill? Perhaps one who enjoys knitting and binge-watching documentaries instead of orchestrating grand heists? Can you imagine a redhead sitting at home with a cup of herbal tea, going, "You know what? I think I'll skip the seduction today and just finish this season of *Planet Earth*." Now that's the kind of representation we could get behind!

Then there are the "quirky best friends," who usually come equipped with an arsenal of one-liners and a penchant for awkward situations. You know the type: the character who's all about "Let's have a spontaneous road trip!" while the rest of the gang is trying to figure out who forgot to pay the gas bill. These characters often provide comic relief, but let's be real—how many of us actually live our lives like that? We don't need to be the ones cracking jokes while the world falls apart around us! Sometimes, we just want to eat ice cream in sweatpants and call it a day.

And let's not forget the "fiery leader" trope, usually a redheaded warrior princess or a rebellious girl fighting against the odds. While it's great to see strong redheaded characters, one has to wonder:

can we have one who doesn't need to slay a dragon or lead a revolution? Maybe she just wants to open a bakery and make the best ginger scones in town. Because honestly, who wouldn't want a redhead wielding a whisk instead of a sword? Imagine the "great battles" she would face: flour flying, recipes exploding, and "whose turn is it to wash the dishes?" arguments raging. Epic!

When we shift our focus to literature, redheads often take center stage as mysterious and passionate characters, embodying the "spirit of fire" trope. Think about it: how many protagonists with red hair are also caught up in wild romances or dramatic adventures? From the spirited Anne of Green Gables to the iconic Ginger Spice, they all share that passionate spark—often leading to love triangles and elaborate plots. But can we also get a redhead who finds joy in gardening or reading at home? Not every fiery character has to be racing against time to save the world!

Let's dive into some classic examples. Anne Shirley, with her trademark braids and vivid imagination, is a beloved character, but she's often portrayed in such a melodramatic light that you'd think she was about to pen the next great tragedy at any moment. And what about that iconic moment when she accidentally dyes her hair green? A nightmare for any redhead, sure, but wouldn't it be refreshing if we saw Anne simply shrug it off and start a new trend? "Green hair? Sure! Who's ready for the next big thing?"

Then we have Ron Weasley from *Harry Potter*, whose red hair serves as a badge of honor among a sea of more muted hues. But let's be honest: Ron's characterization often feels like it comes with a side of "comic relief." Sure, he's brave and loyal, but how about a Ron who takes center stage for a moment and shows us that redheads can have moments of grace and wisdom too? Picture him as the wise sage, giving advice while expertly brewing potions (without the help of Hermione, thank you very much). "Ah, yes, the secret to perfect potion brewing lies not just in the ingredients, but in the soul of the redhead!"

As for animated characters, there's Merida from *Brave*, who takes the "fiery" title to heart, complete with archery skills and a rebellious spirit. But is it too much to ask for a redhead who simply wants to enjoy a day at the spa? "Forget the bears and the bow-and-arrow skills; I just want to sip tea and get a facial!"

Let's take a stroll down memory lane and look at how redheads have fared in older films and literature. The classic Disney princesses usually have their locks in shades of blonde or black, with the occasional brunette. But along comes Ariel from *The Little Mermaid*, a true trailblazer! She broke the mold, combining an adventurous spirit with a fiery mane. Yet, what's her journey all about? Trading her voice for legs! Maybe we should have a new story where a redhead trades her beauty for... I don't know, a free lifetime supply of pizza? Talk about a twist!

Then there's the beloved Pippi Longstocking, a character whose hair is as wild as her spirit. Pippi embodies the essence of carefree living, but let's be real: how many of us have the energy to spend every day on a new adventure? "Today, I'll go treasure hunting! Tomorrow, I'll conquer the seas!" Meanwhile, most of us are just hoping to finish that one book we started last summer.

As we venture into the realm of social media, we see redheads banding together to discuss their portrayals in pop culture. Facebook groups like "Redhead Memes" are filled with amusing anecdotes and commentary. One member might share a funny story about their grandmother, who always insisted that their family heritage could be traced back to some fiery-haired Viking ancestor. "Of course," they might joke, "I inherited the hair and the penchant for mischief but missed out on the whole conquering villages part." It's in these conversations that we find community, shared laughter, and an understanding that while the media might not always get it right, we're here to embrace our unique identities.

But let's not ignore the positive impacts of representation. When redheads are portrayed in diverse ways—whether as scholars, quirky artists, or hilarious goofballs—it helps to broaden the understanding of who we are. It allows redheads everywhere to feel like they belong to a larger narrative, one that celebrates their uniqueness without forcing them into a box labeled "fiery" or "troublemaker."

The truth is, redheads have always been a vibrant part of storytelling, bringing a splash of color and a hint of chaos wherever they go. Whether we're leading epic quests or simply enjoying a quiet evening in, the redhead narrative is evolving. Here's hoping for more tales that showcase our many shades—because who wouldn't want a little extra spice in their life?

Adult Bullies

With locks that shimmer like a fiery sunset, we're not just walking around; we're practically a walking advertisement for a hair dye company. But let's not sugarcoat it: our unique hue can sometimes bring out the green-eyed monster in others. Yes, jealousy is a real thing, and apparently, it doesn't just live in high school hallways. Nope, it can thrive among adults, too—just ask any redhead who's been playfully bullied by their peers.

Now, don't get me wrong; I'm all for healthy competition. I mean, if someone wants to strut around with their luxurious brunette mane or their sun-kissed blonde locks, more power to them! But when that competition turns into snarky comments and unsolicited opinions, we might just have to throw down a gauntlet of ginger fury.

Picture this: you walk into a room filled with a group of well-coiffed adults, and the moment you enter, you can practically hear the collective thoughts. "Did you see her hair? It's like she's trying to steal all the attention!" Yes, Janet, I know my hair is vibrant. Thank you for pointing it out like I'm a circus act. But the truth is, I'm just as much of a hot mess as anyone else. I didn't wake up like this on purpose—if I had, I'd have at least coordinated my outfit!

Let's dive into the psyche of the non-redhead. They see a fiery mane and suddenly feel the need to comment. "Oh, you have red hair! I could never pull that off!" they exclaim, as if red hair comes with a warning label. "Caution: Wearer may attract attention and cause envy." Meanwhile, you're just standing there, minding your own business, and contemplating whether it's socially acceptable to wear sweatpants to a party.

And then there are the adult bullies. Yes, they exist. Picture a group of friends sitting around a table, sipping their lattes, and suddenly you hear, "Why does she get to wear that color? It looks terrible on anyone else!" This comment is often accompanied by a chorus of nodding heads. Yes, folks, you can be bullied by grown adults who clearly have too much time on their hands—and probably an unhealthy obsession with their own hair color.

You know you've hit peak jealousy when someone dramatically throws their head back and exclaims,

"I wish I had red hair! But, you know, only if it looked like that." Cue the exaggerated eye-roll and the side-eye glances. This is the adult version of the classic schoolyard taunt: "I'm not jealous; I just think your hair looks like a traffic cone!"

So, what gives? Why does my fabulous hair color evoke such a visceral reaction? Is it the fear of being outshone, or do they just really believe that the world is running out of available shades of dye? Perhaps it's a little bit of both. After all, every time I step into a room, I can practically hear the gears turning in their heads: "Is it too late for me to dye my hair that color? Should I have gone for the 'fiery red' or just stuck with my mundane brown?"

But let's be real—being a redhead isn't just about commanding attention or invoking jealousy; it's about owning your uniqueness. Sure, you might have to deal with the occasional jealous jab from Janet or her crew, but you also get to strut your stuff like you're walking down a runway every day. And when it comes to color, red is more than just a hue; it's a badge of honor.

You might think this is a teenage phenomenon reserved for high school lunch tables, but oh no, my friend, it's alive and thriving in the grown-up world. Welcome to the jungle!

Let's set the scene. You're at a networking event, dressed to the nines, and your hair is catching the light like it's auditioning for a shampoo commercial. You can feel the stares. The murmurs. And, of course, the whispers of "Who does she think she is?" It's like a chorus of envy with a side of confusion. The non-redheads in the room seem torn between admiration and the urge to either compliment you or throw a drink in your face. It's a delicate balance!

You wander over to the snack table, thinking that maybe some hors d'oeuvres will help ease the tension. But the moment you reach for the last shrimp cocktail, you hear it—the unmistakable sound of a non-redhead's voice dripping with jealousy. "Wow, she really thinks she can just waltz in here and take the last shrimp, doesn't she?"

Oh, come on, Karen! It's a shrimp, not the Holy Grail! But, alas, the drama unfolds. The next thing you know, you're being eyed like a contestant on a reality show. "Will she or won't she?" you think. Should you toss the shrimp back and walk away like a saint, or take a bite and own your fabulousness?

Then there's the classic workplace scenario. Picture this: it's Monday morning, and everyone's dragging their feet. You stroll in, radiating energy (and, okay, maybe a little hair gel), and suddenly the office transforms. "Who invited the walking highlighter?" mutters your coworker, Susan, under her breath, as she tries to style her flat brown hair into a messy bun for the umpteenth time.

You'd think that in an environment filled with deadlines and spreadsheets, the focus would be on actual work, right? Nope! Instead, you become the unofficial subject of the office gossip. "Did you see how she wore that fiery red dress? So dramatic!" Yes, Susan, it's called having a personality, but I'm glad you noticed!

What's even funnier is how some people will go out of their way to create scenarios where they can critique your style choices. "Oh, I would never wear that shade of red; it's just so… intense." Intense? Honey, it's called confidence! But who has time to unpack that when there's an endless supply of side-eye glances to manage?

Let's not forget the friends who suddenly turn into fashion critics. You might be out for a fun night, wearing that killer outfit that makes you feel like a million bucks. Then one of your friends, perhaps with slightly less vibrant locks, leans over and says, "You know, I just don't think red is your color."

Um, excuse me? Is it too bright for you, or do you just prefer the muted palette of your own wardrobe? This is the same friend who, while scrolling through social media, will gush about how much she loves "unique colors" but has never had the courage to step outside her own neutral comfort zone.

And just when you think you've escaped the judgment, you hear it: "You know, I think red hair is only for a certain type of person." What does that even mean? Does a specific hair color come with a manual on who can wear it? Are there secret meetings where only the boldest among us can gather and discuss our hair hue eligibility?

Yet, for all the jealousy and snarky remarks, there's also a certain camaraderie that forms among redheads. When we spot one another across a crowded room, it's like an unspoken bond—a secret club where we acknowledge our shared experiences. "Look at her! Isn't she fabulous?" we think. There's a sense of mutual respect, knowing we all face the same peculiarities that come with being red-haired in a world of browns and blondes.

Picture this: you're at a summer barbecue, sipping on a fancy drink adorned with a tiny umbrella. You notice a fellow redhead across the yard, and suddenly it feels like you're both in on a secret that no one else understands. It's like a scene straight out of a rom-com where two unlikely heroes find each other amidst a sea of ordinary folks. You exchange knowing glances, and just like that, you're bonded for life.

"Is it just me, or do they seem threatened by us?" she asks, motioning to the non-redheads trying too hard to be friendly while subtly adjusting their own hair to a more subdued hue. You both laugh, realizing that you've hit upon a universal truth: redheads have a unique allure that can spark envy in even the friendliest of faces.

Now, let's not underestimate the power of the shared experience. When redheads gather—be it at a themed party, a festival, or even a casual coffee meetup—there's an instant connection. Conversations flow easily, filled with tales of hair dye disasters, wardrobe malfunctions involving clashing colors, and hilarious encounters with jealous onlookers. "Remember that time someone asked if my hair was natural, and I said yes, and then they just stared at me like I was an alien?" Classic!

It's also in these gatherings that we learn to navigate jealousy in a supportive way. Rather than letting envy create a divide, redheads tend to uplift one another. Compliments fly like confetti: "That shade of red is stunning! Where did you get that lipstick?" It's a beautiful exchange where jealousy transforms into admiration and support.

Of course, let's not forget the joy of creating memes and social media groups dedicated to redhead experiences. You'd be amazed at the cathartic power of sharing funny posts about the daily struggles of having bright hair and pale skin. The "Redhead Memes" Facebook group is a treasure trove of humor where redheads come together to share everything from hair care tips to the best sunscreen for our sensitive skin. One member recently shared a hilarious story about her grandmother's fiery locks and how her ancestors were considered witches—who knew we had such magical lineage?

And then there's the ultimate bonding experience: attending events specifically for redheads. Yes, they exist, and yes, they are as amazing as they sound. From redhead festivals to "Ginger Gatherings," these events celebrate our unique identities and create a sense of community that's hard to replicate elsewhere. Imagine a sea of red hair swaying in the breeze, laughter ringing through the air as you share stories of surviving the stares and whispers.

These events are often filled with playful competitions, like "Best Redhead Hair Flip" and "Most Creative Use of Accessories with Red Hair." You'll find yourself cheering for fellow redheads as if you're at the Olympics, because let's face it: we deserve a gold medal for living life in a world where our hair color can spark either awe or envy!

So, how do we navigate the jealousy of others while embracing our vibrant community? By creating spaces where support outweighs envy. When we see non-redheads experiencing a pang of jealousy, let's extend an olive branch (or maybe just a compliment) instead of fanning the flames.

The Fire Within

Let's dive into the personality traits often associated with our kind, which, spoiler alert, usually include passion, fierceness, and humor.

First up, passion. Now, you might think, "Oh great, another redhead who's into dramatic monologues about the environment!" But let's not stereotype too quickly. Yes, we do have a tendency to get excited about causes—be it saving the planet or advocating for the right shade of lipstick. Seriously, if you've ever met a redhead in a discussion about climate change, you might as well grab a front-row seat because it's going to be an emotional rollercoaster! We talk with our hands, our eyes light up, and before you know it, we've recruited half the room to join our cause.

You can spot a passionate redhead by their ability to make any conversation sound like a TED Talk.

"What's that? You love pizza? Let me tell you about the environmental impact of cheese production!" It's a gift, really. We can turn a casual chat about toppings into a full-fledged debate on the ethical implications of pepperoni.

Next on the list is fierceness. Oh boy, do we wear this one like a badge of honor! Whether we're defending our favorite ice cream flavor or standing up for our friends in a heated debate, redheads have a certain tenacity that can rival a lion protecting its cubs. And let's be honest, when we get fired up, it's like watching a firework show—bright, loud, and maybe a little alarming.

I once saw a fellow redhead confront a guy who accidentally stepped on her shoe at a concert. It was as if she had transformed into a superhero—"Fear not, for I am here to defend the sanctity of my footwear!" She delivered a monologue that would have made Shakespeare weep. "You shall not tread upon these glorious crimson creations without consequence!" And let me tell you, by the end, the guy was apologizing profusely, promising to never wear shoes again if it meant preventing a redhead's wrath.

But let's not forget the most delightful trait of all: humor. Redheads have a unique ability to turn any situation into a comedic skit. Got dumped? Well, there's a Netflix special waiting to happen! We laugh at our own misfortunes because, let's face it, life's too short to take seriously—especially when you have hair that attracts more attention than a celebrity at a red carpet event.

Take, for example, the infamous "redhead jokes." Oh, we know them all. "Why do redheads make terrible detectives? Because they always stick out like a sore thumb!" Sure, it's a cliché, but it gives us the perfect opportunity to turn the tables. "Well, at least I'm not going to be overlooked in a crowd! What's your excuse?"

In all seriousness, our humor is often a coping mechanism. It helps us deflect the occasional weird stares or the unsolicited comments from strangers who seem to think our hair color gives them a license to ask bizarre questions. "Is it true redheads have more fun?" Yes, indeed! But we also have to deal with weirdness—like when someone assumes that we spontaneously combust when exposed to sunlight.

Let's start with the big one: the "fiery temper." Now, let's be real here. Yes, we might have a reputation for being a tad intense, but is it really our fault that we're passionate about everything? When a redhead gets angry, it's like watching a volcano prepare to erupt. You can see the buildup, you can feel the tension in the air, and if you're smart, you'll have an escape plan ready. But hey, it's not all bad!

Being "fiery" means we bring that same passion to everything we do, from fighting for social justice to defending our favorite TV shows. When we're on board with something, we are all in, like someone who's just discovered an all-you-can-eat ice cream bar. This can lead to some of the most spirited discussions, debates, and yes, occasional shouting matches. But let's face it: that energy can also create some of the most vibrant and memorable experiences.

Consider the classic "redhead at a karaoke night" scenario. When a redhead steps up to the mic, you know you're in for a show. Whether it's belting out a power ballad or performing an interpretive dance to a pop hit, we don't just sing—we perform! Friends will be cheering, and strangers will be both mesmerized and mildly terrified, like they've just witnessed a lion tamer doing a tap dance in the middle of a circus ring.

Now, onto the next stereotype: the "seductive redhead." Oh yes, the trope that redheads are mysterious, alluring, and a touch dangerous. I mean, come on! Have you ever tried to seduce someone while your hair color screams "LOOK AT ME"? It's like trying to hide an elephant in a room full of mice. And yet, we embrace it, donning that reputation like a fabulous cape, ready to strut into the room and capture attention.

But with great allure comes great responsibility. Navigating the dating scene can sometimes feel like a high-stakes game of dodgeball. You walk into a bar, and suddenly all eyes are on you—not just because of your hair, but because people are trying to figure out if you're going to be the enchanting redhead who sweeps them off their feet or the one who accidentally sets the bar on fire with your charm.

And then there are the odd comments. "Oh, you must be fiery in bed!" they say, as if we're all auditioning for a role in a romantic thriller. Really? I just wanted to enjoy my drink in peace! But hey, we take it in stride, armed with a sense of humor and a cheeky comeback. "Oh, honey, if you think my hair is the only thing that's fiery, you clearly underestimate how well I can extinguish unwanted attention." Yes, this really happened.

Now, while living up to these stereotypes can sometimes be fun, it can also lead to some rather awkward situations. Ever had a well-meaning friend say, "You're so passionate! You should totally start a club!"? Congratulations! You've just been nominated president of a society that may or may not involve glitter and spontaneous dance-offs.

Then there's the pressure to constantly embody these traits. When you're a redhead, it feels like you're expected to be the life of the party, the firecracker in the group, the one who brings the enthusiasm. But what happens when you're just having a "meh" day? Sometimes, the world needs a quiet redhead who just wants to binge-watch a series in peace. Yet, you're still the one people expect to lead the karaoke night.

But here's the kicker: it's okay to break the mold. While stereotypes can be fun, they shouldn't define us. As redheads, we're allowed to embrace our fiery spirit when we feel like it, but we're equally allowed to be chill, goofy, or downright quirky when the mood strikes.

First, let's talk about the infamous "redhead privilege." Yes, it exists! When you walk into a room, heads turn like you're walking on a catwalk, and you might as well be wearing a crown. People will approach you with compliments that range from genuine admiration to sheer disbelief: "Wow, your hair is so bright! Do you get your color from a bottle, or did you just wrestle with a fire hydrant?"

And then there's the classic line: "You must be a fun person!" It's almost like a rite of passage for redheads. But here's the kicker—while we might be known for our vibrant personalities, sometimes we just want to sip our coffee in peace, preferably while scrolling through memes about cats. But no! The world demands our energy! So, we put on our best "fun" face and prepare for the onslaught of questions about our hair care routine, as if we're hiding the secret formula for world peace in our conditioner.

Speaking of hair care, let's take a moment to appreciate the wild and wacky world of redhead hair products. If you're not careful, you can end up with a cabinet full of colorful bottles that look like they belong in a rainbow factory. There's the "fiery red" shampoo, the "sunset glow" conditioner, and let's not forget the "high-octane shine spray" that promises to make you look like you just walked out of a shampoo commercial. Pro tip: avoid using the shine spray before a first date unless you want to give your date the impression that they're sitting next to a disco ball.

Now, let's address the elephant in the room: jealousy from non-redheads. It's real, folks! There's something about our vibrant locks that can spark a bit of envy, leading to awkward encounters. You might find yourself in a conversation where a non-redhead insists, "I just don't get it! How do you pull off that color? It's so... bright!" Well, my friend, it's a gift and a curse. But hey, at least they're noticing, right?

And let's not forget the side-eye we get from parents at the playground. You know the ones—those moms with perfectly coordinated outfits and hair that has clearly never faced a gust of wind. They'll look at you, then at their kids, and you can practically hear them thinking, "Will my child turn out like her?!" Calm down, Karen; I'm just here for the free cookies and a good laugh!

Then, there's the delightful world of online memes and jokes about being a redhead. Have you ever been part of a "Redhead Memes" group? It's like a sanctuary where we can all come together and laugh about the little things, from our struggles to find matching hair ties to the eternal search for the right foundation shade that doesn't make us look like we've just come back from a trip to the moon.

One meme that particularly struck a chord was about how redheads are "like the unicorns of hair colors" — rare, fabulous, and often confused about how to blend in with the normal, non-magical folks.

But let's also take a moment to appreciate the beauty of the bond we share as redheads. It's like having a built-in support group. Whether you're at a gathering or online, you can swap stories about the time someone mistook your hair for a light bulb or the infamous "How do you get your hair that color?" question. It's comforting to know you're not alone in the world of fiery hair and passionate personalities.

And speaking of gatherings, let's not overlook the fun events we get to attend! Whether it's a "Redhead Day" festival in the Netherlands or a local meetup at a coffee shop, there's something special about being surrounded by fellow redheads. You can laugh, share tips on the best hair products, and even debate whether or not you can wear pink without looking like a walking cotton candy stand.

Fake or Brake?

Ah, Elizabethan England—a time of ruffles, court intrigue, and hair that could only be described as a serious commitment. While most of us struggle to get through a week without a trip to the salon, the Elizabethans had a whole different vibe. Hair was not just hair; it was a status symbol, a conversation starter, and occasionally, a fire hazard. And at the top of this flamboyant hair hierarchy? Red wigs, of course.

Imagine walking into a banquet hall in 16th-century London, where the air is thick with the scent of roasted meats and the laughter of nobles. But wait—what's that? The unmistakable sight of a bright red wig bobbing around, making waves like a celebrity on a red carpet. Queen Elizabeth I herself was a major influencer in this realm, sporting a magnificent red wig that would make even the fiercest fashionista envious. When your royal hairstyle could double as a battle helmet, you know you've made it.

But let's not forget the wig makers—the unsung heroes of the time. These artisans were not only tasked with crafting hairpieces that would make even the dullest noble shine; they had to contend with an unexpected challenge: achieving the perfect shade of red. "Is it too bright? Too muted? Or does it look like a cherry exploded on a cloudy day?" The pressure was on. After all, you couldn't just pop down to the local beauty supply store. A bad wig could lead to whispers of witchcraft, and nobody wanted to end up on the wrong side of a witch trial.

And speaking of trials, let's dive into the fascinating world of societal perceptions. In this era, red hair was often associated with fierce qualities—think passion, ambition, and an inclination to duel. People would say, "Look at her hair! She must be fiery in spirit!" Little did they know, a redhead's true fieriness might actually be a result of an unfortunate sunburn and a poorly timed visit to the pub.

Of course, red-haired individuals often attracted their fair share of attention—sometimes good, sometimes bad. While some admirers might be enamored by the fiery locks, others could view a redhead with suspicion, whispering about witchcraft or, heaven forbid, unruly behavior. You know the stereotype: "Redheads are just a bit too much." But then again, "too much" was the entire point of Elizabethan fashion. If your outfit didn't leave a trail of gasps in its wake, what was the point?

Fast forward to today, and the charm of red hair continues to captivate. Whether it's a natural hue or a vibrant dye job, red hair remains a striking choice, one that many aspire to—especially those childhood bullies who once made your life miserable for being different. Oh, the irony! Those same kids who teased you for your "fiery" locks now show up at high school reunions sporting the most eye-popping shades of red imaginable, like they just stepped off the set of a rom-com about hair dye disasters. "Oh, look who decided to embrace their inner ginger!" you might chuckle, knowing full well that they'd once claimed they'd never date a redhead.

But what about those authentic red wigs? As we'll explore later, wig makers today face their own struggles, particularly when it comes to creating natural-looking red wigs for children undergoing cancer treatment. In a world that often overlooks the struggles behind the scenes, these artisans and their craft hold profound meaning, reminding us that hair—whether real or wigged—can symbolize more than just beauty; it can represent strength, resilience, and community.

In the Elizabethan era, if you wanted to go red, you had to get creative. Forget about the fancy chemical concoctions we have today. Back then, you might find yourself in a chemist's lab, mixing up a potion that could either result in a fabulous fiery hue or leave you looking like you just survived a battle with a rogue beet. The ingredients? Often a combination of plants, minerals, and maybe even a dash of dragon's blood—though I suspect that was mostly just an overzealous marketing ploy.

Now, let's talk about the royal enthusiasts of red hair. When Queen Elizabeth I strutted around with her golden-red tresses, she wasn't just making a fashion statement; she was creating a whole brand. That's right—Elizabeth was the original influencer, turning heads and making the rest of the court green with envy. You can just imagine the gossip: "Did you see what Liz is rocking today? It's like a sunset on fire! I heard she mixed a new dye from crushed beetles and a hint of lemon zest."

But alas, not everyone had the privilege of royal hair care. For the common folk, achieving that coveted red was more akin to a game of chance. Many a villager would end up with hair that was, shall we say, less than ideal. Picture a farmer emerging from the dye shop, only to be greeted with laughter from the townsfolk. "Look! Farmer Bob's gone full lobster again! Someone get him a bib!"

Fast forward to the 18th century, and things didn't improve much. While wigs became all the rage, people still wanted to get in on the red action. The problem? Dyes were notoriously unreliable. One wrong move, and you could emerge looking like a poorly cooked crab instead of the dazzling redhead you envisioned. "Did you say 'fabulous' or 'flambé'?" became a common refrain among those brave enough to try.

Enter the modern age, where hair dye has become an art form, a science, and an excuse for a midlife crisis all rolled into one. Who knew that those childhood bullies would grow up and suddenly become hair dye aficionados, transforming themselves into red-haired wonders? It's as if they collectively decided, "Hey, let's reclaim the hair color we once mocked!" While they flaunt their new crimson locks, you can't help but smirk, thinking about how they once swore they'd never date a redhead. Oh, the irony!

Now, let's address the elephant in the room—or should I say the wig in the corner? Red wigs today are often the topic of heated debate among those who seek the perfect shade. "This one looks too orange! This one looks like I've been rolling around in a pile of autumn leaves!" The quest for the ideal red wig has become a saga worthy of its own epic tale. Some wig makers even admit that their biggest challenge is creating something that doesn't look like a Halloween costume gone awry.

And speaking of challenges, we can't overlook the incredible artisans who work hard to craft natural-looking wigs for children battling cancer. Their dedication is nothing short of inspiring. As these wig makers strive to provide beautiful options for young ones who have lost their hair, they ensure that the spirit of red remains alive and well. If you think about it, the children sporting these wigs are not just wearing hair; they're wearing a badge of courage, with each vibrant strand representing hope, resilience, and the sass that only a redhead can embody.

In today's society, red hair isn't just a pigment; it's a movement. From TikTok challenges featuring "Redhead Hair Goals" to Instagram influencers flaunting their flame-colored locks with unapologetic pride, redheads are everywhere! You'd think there was a secret underground society dedicated to the pursuit of fiery tresses—and honestly, there might just be. If you hear whispers of a "Redhead Revolution," grab your besties and your brightest wigs, because it's party time!

One of the most amusing aspects of this modern redhead renaissance is the camaraderie that has sprung up among those with fiery manes. Ever been to a gathering of redheads? It's like stepping into a carnival of color, where everyone shares their hair dye mishaps and wig triumphs. "Remember that time I tried to go bright crimson and ended up looking like I was auditioning for a role in a horror movie?" Ah, yes, the great Hair Color Catastrophe of 2022. If only there had been a reality show to document those tragic attempts—"Extreme Hair Makeovers: Redhead Edition."

And let's not forget the wonderful social media groups where redheads gather to swap stories, share tips, and celebrate their unique heritage. Take the "Redhead Memes" Facebook group, for instance. Here, you'll find everything from memes about the perils of being a redhead to heartwarming tales of ancestry. It's like a digital family reunion—one where everyone knows the struggle of being mistaken for a leprechaun on St. Patrick's Day. "No, I don't have a pot of gold, but I do have fabulous hair!"

As redheads continue to make their mark in literature, film, and fashion, they also challenge stereotypes. Gone are the days when a fiery mane meant you had to be feisty or temperamental. Redheads today can be fierce leaders, hilarious comedians, and even soft-hearted romantics—all while rocking their signature color. Just imagine a boardroom filled with red-haired executives, passionately debating the next big marketing strategy. "I say we go bold! Like my hair!" It's a scene that could make anyone proud to be part of the redhead legacy.

146

Aging Gracefully

We don't age like mere mortals.

From the moment we popped into this world, sporting those vibrant locks, it was clear we weren't just another face in the crowd. Oh no, we were like a walking advertisement for the crayon box that everyone secretly wished they had. "Can I borrow your hair for my art project?" was a question I heard more than once. Little did they know, my hair was as temperamental as a toddler after skipping nap time.

School was a special kind of jungle, where every day was a chance for someone to either fawn over your "gorgeous" hair or use it as fodder for the latest playground roast. You could practically set your watch by the arrival of the morning bullying brigade, armed with their arsenal of snide remarks.

"Does the carpet match the drapes?" they'd giggle, clearly unaware that the only thing matching was their lack of creativity.

In the early years, I found comfort in my family's affection for my hair color. My mom often said, "You were meant to stand out, darling." Which was lovely and all, but a little support wouldn't have hurt when I had to endure my classmate's attempts to "find the rainbow" in my hair—like it was some kind of scavenger hunt gone horribly wrong.

Let's not forget the hair care rituals my parents put me through. The sheer volume of conditioner required to manage those fiery tresses could probably fund a small country. "Honey, we can't go out until we detangle the dragon!" my mom would exclaim, wielding a brush like a sword. And honestly, by the time I was ready for school, I looked less like a child and more like a particularly fiery lion from the Savannah.

And then there were the magical hair products. Enter the world of "special redhead shampoos"—a marketing ploy designed to convince kids that their hair was a rare artifact needing its own museum. The labels promised to enhance vibrancy, prevent fading, and even protect against the sun. Spoiler alert: they did none of these things. Instead, I often ended up with hair that resembled a warning sign for impending thunderstorms.

Teenhood brings a whole new level of scrutiny. Suddenly, it's not just about whether your hair is bright red or just slightly more orange than the rest of the crayon box. Nope, now it's about hair highlights, lowlights, and whether your color is "on trend." The pressure was real, and there I was, faced with the ultimate dilemma: to dye or not to dye?

Enter the teenage girls' sacred ritual of hair dyeing parties, where friends gathered armed with bottles of dye, questionable music choices, and a shared belief that turning your hair a vibrant shade of purple would somehow solve all your problems. "Just think how fabulous you'll look!" they'd insist. I often found myself staring at the mirror, wondering if I really wanted to risk resembling a grape-flavored popsicle.

Then came the inevitable peer pressure. "Why don't you try something fun? You know, like brown or blonde?" the well-meaning friends would chirp. As if transforming from a fiery beacon to a color that resembled oatmeal was a logical step in my evolution! Little did they know, I was fiercely loyal to my red roots.

But teenage life isn't all about hair drama; it's also filled with awkward crushes and crush-worthy moments. There's nothing quite like a crush who suddenly notices you because of your vibrant hair. "Wow, I love your hair! It's so... red," they'd stammer, clearly flustered. You'd think my hair had magical powers, the way it sent hearts racing. The only problem? I'd inevitably trip over my own feet trying to respond.

Then there's the inevitable run-in with jealousy. While I was blessed with these gorgeous locks, I quickly learned that not everyone was thrilled about it. Picture this: a group of girls glaring from the corner of the cafeteria, muttering about how unfair it was that I got all the attention. I'd roll my eyes and joke to my friends, "Oh please, I'm just here to eat my salad, not steal your spotlight!" But deep down, it stung like a freshly plucked hair.

High school also brought its own unique set of challenges: gym class. I can't tell you how many times I was singled out for the "crazy redhead" persona during team sports. "Go for the fiery one!" the coach would shout, as if I were some kind of wild animal that could run circles around everyone. Spoiler alert: I was just as coordinated as a newborn deer on roller skates.

And let's talk about hair care routines, shall we? The quest for the perfect shampoo became a full-time job. Suddenly, there were products claiming to be "redhead-friendly," promising to enhance vibrancy while promising the elusive "non-fade formula." I felt like a scientist in a lab, testing everything from herbal remedies to questionable concoctions that left my hair smelling like a salad bar.

As prom season rolled around, so did the inevitable "what color should I wear?" dilemma. Should I go with a daring emerald green to match my hair, or should I risk looking like I wandered out of a box of crayons? It was a toss-up between "fashionista" and "fire hazard," and let's be honest, who doesn't want to look like they've just escaped a fashionable inferno?

Amidst all the chaos, teenage years also gave us a sense of belonging. There was an unspoken bond among redheads, like a secret club where we shared knowing glances and laughter about our vibrant hues. In those moments, it became clear: no matter how tumultuous this time was, we were in it together.

By the time we threw our caps in the air at graduation, it was clear that our fiery hair had not only become a signature look but also a badge of honor. We had survived the teenage tempest, and while our hair might have changed, the confidence we forged during those years would be our greatest asset moving forward.

Remember the carefree days of youth? Well, say goodbye to those as you navigate the rollercoaster of jobs, relationships, and existential crises—all while trying to maintain your vibrant red locks.

Let's kick things off with the workplace. Suddenly, your hair isn't just a fabulous accessory; it's a potential conversation starter, a confidence booster, and occasionally, a source of office envy. "Wow, you must be a firecracker in meetings!" someone will say, as if the color of your hair has anything to do with your ability to balance spreadsheets. Newsflash: just because I have red hair doesn't mean I'll turn into a fiery beast during negotiations. I'm more of a "let's discuss this over coffee" type, with maybe a dash of passive-aggressive Post-it notes on the side.

Then there's the dilemma of dating. As a redhead, you quickly realize that your hair color often attracts attention—both good and bad. "I love redheads!" your dates might declare, as if you're a rare breed of unicorn instead of a human being just trying to figure out where to eat dinner. But be prepared for the flip side: "You must be fiery in bed!" is the classic line that makes you wish for a bucket of cold water to douse their enthusiasm. Really? Because I assure you, my passion level doesn't correlate with my hair color!

Navigating relationships is like trying to dye your hair without getting any on your skin: messy and fraught with challenges. You'll find yourself on awkward first dates, where you have to endure endless questions about your hair. "So, do you get your hair color from a bottle?" they'll ask, trying to be clever. As if I'd say, "Yes, I bought it at the grocery store in the aisle next to the ketchup!"

As adulthood continues, there's the reality of maintenance. Hair dyeing becomes a scheduled event, akin to a dentist appointment. You'll find yourself Googling "best red hair dye" at 2 a.m., wondering if you should splurge on the fancy brand or stick with the drugstore option. And don't even get me started on the struggle of finding a good stylist! "I want to keep my red vibrant but not clownish," you'll say, only to have them nod while secretly planning a bright cherry makeover that leaves you looking like a walking advertisement for a candy shop.

And here's a twist: remember those childhood bullies who teased you? You'll find that many of them grow up to dye their hair red, as if they suddenly discovered that they, too, wanted to be a "fiery goddess." You might catch them at the grocery store, casually flipping their new crimson locks while avoiding eye contact. "Oh, look who decided to join the redhead club!" you might think, suppressing a laugh as they pretend they've always admired your fabulous hair. Ah, the sweet taste of irony.

But with adulthood comes the reality of aging—your hair color might change whether you like it or not. As time marches on, you might find yourself discovering strands of silver amidst your fiery mane. While some might panic and reach for the dye, I say embrace it! After all, those silver strands can add a sophisticated flair, like a finely aged wine or that vintage leather jacket you've been eyeing.

The social scene also evolves. Instead of carefree gatherings, you're now attending events that involve "networking" and "professional connections," where casual hair is replaced with sleek styles and business attire. But even in the most formal of settings, you'll spot fellow redheads, and it feels like a secret handshake. A nod here, a compliment there, and suddenly, you're sharing stories about the best hair products and commiserating over the struggles of maintaining the perfect shade.

Through it all—awkward dates, workplace quirks, and the aging process—being a redhead remains a part of your identity. You learn to own it, to flaunt it, and even to laugh at the ridiculousness of it all. You might even find a certain pride in being the "fiery one" in your friend group, a title you wear like a badge.

Red Legacy

Throughout history, we redheads have often stolen the spotlight—both literally and figuratively. From fierce warriors to iconic entertainers, our fiery locks have not only made us stand out in a crowd but have also played significant roles in shaping culture and society. With a blend of charisma, talent, and sometimes a dash of madness, we famous redheads have left indelible marks on the pages of history. So, let's grab our favorite shade of lipstick (preferably a vibrant red) as we journey through time to meet some remarkable redheads and explore our contributions—because who knew red hair could come with so much pizzazz?

Let's start with the classic icon of the fiery redhead: Queen Elizabeth I of England. The "Virgin Queen" was not only known for her impressive rule but also for her legendary mane. With hair as bright as her political ambitions, she sported a look that inspired countless artists and made her a symbol of power and femininity. Her decision to flaunt her red locks was strategic, a bold statement that helped solidify her identity. Who wouldn't want to rule a kingdom while rocking hair that could double as a warning signal? "Watch out, enemies! This queen has a fierce look and a stronger will!"

Moving on from royalty to the realm of literature, we encounter the enchanting character of Anne of Green Gables. Created by Canadian author L.M. Montgomery, Anne Shirley is the quintessential literary redhead—imaginative, spirited, and, let's be honest, prone to a bit of drama. With her fiery hair and even fierier temper, she became a beloved figure in children's literature. Anne taught us the power of imagination and the importance of being unapologetically ourselves. Plus, her adventures showed us that sometimes, life is just a series of delightful disasters waiting to happen—preferably with a side of raspberry cordial.

As we journey further through history, we come to a trailblazing redhead who changed the face of cinema: Lucille Ball. The queen of comedy, we redheads know Ball was not just a hilarious actress; she was a pioneer in the television industry. With her signature red hair and unmatched comedic timing, she brought joy to countless households. "I Love Lucy" became a cultural phenomenon, and her portrayal of the lovable Lucy Ricardo showcased the beauty of imperfect life—because who hasn't tried to hide a loaf of bread under their hat? Her legacy continues to influence comedians and actors today, proving that laughter really is the best medicine—even if it sometimes comes with a side of chaos.

Speaking of chaos, let's not forget the red-haired powerhouse of rock and roll: Mick Jagger. The Rolling Stones frontman is more than just a musical legend; he's a cultural icon. With his wild hair and even wilder stage presence, Jagger captivated audiences and helped shape the sound of a generation. He taught us that it's okay to be a little outrageous—preferably while dancing like no one is watching, even if everyone is indeed watching (and taking videos for Instagram). Jagger's influence transcends music; he represents a lifestyle of rebellion, passion, and unapologetic self-expression. Just don't ask him to perform in a quiet coffee shop—he might scare the baristas with those signature moves!

Then there's the world of politics, where redheads have occasionally stirred things up. Take Winston Churchill, for instance. While known for his remarkable leadership during World War II, he was also famous for his fiery red hair in his youth. Churchill's tenacity and determination helped rally a nation during dark times. His speeches ignited hope and courage, proving that even a redhead can inspire resilience in the face of adversity. Plus, he had a way of making a cigar look fashionable—talk about multitasking!

In more contemporary times, we see the rise of redheaded icons like Emma Stone and Amy Adams, who have both graced the big screen with their talent and, yes, their fabulous hair. Stone, with her dazzling red locks, has become a symbol of versatility in Hollywood, winning hearts and awards alike. Meanwhile, Adams has charmed audiences with her performances, reminding us that red hair can also bring a touch of sweetness and warmth to any role. Both actresses showcase the range of redhead representation, demonstrating that being a redhead is about more than just fiery locks; it's about the heart and humor we bring to the table.

Throughout the ages, we redheads have faced our fair share of challenges, often navigating stereotypes that paint us as fiery or temperamental. However, many of us have turned these misconceptions into powerful narratives, reshaping our identities and inspiring others. Whether we've been seen as witchy figures in folklore or as passionate individuals in popular media, we have consistently defied expectations.

Culturally, the redhead trope has evolved, shedding outdated notions while embracing new dimensions of identity. From fashion to art to literature, we continue to influence trends and inspire creativity. The embrace of individuality—whether through hair color or personality—reminds us that everyone can find their place in the world, even if they do happen to stand out like a flamingo in a flock of pigeons.

It's clear that our impact on culture and society has been nothing short of remarkable. From queens to comedians, from politicians to rock stars, we redheads have left our mark with flair, passion, and a touch of humor. So, the next time you spot a redhead, whether in a book, on screen, or walking down the street, remember the legacy we carry—a legacy that celebrates individuality, creativity, and the undeniable truth that sometimes, it really is good to be a redhead.

Passing the Torch

As we look to the next generation of redheads, it's hard not to feel a mix of nostalgia and excitement. Nostalgia, because we remember those awkward teenage years when our fiery locks set us apart—often resulting in bewildered stares, questionable comments, and that time we tried to dye our hair "normal" only to end up looking like a malfunctioning traffic light. And excitement, because today's young redheads are stepping into a world where their vibrant identities can shine brighter than ever. So, let's dive into some lighthearted advice for the fiery-haired youth of tomorrow, who will undoubtedly inherit our legacy of sass and charm.

First things first: embrace the hair! Red hair is like a superhero cape—powerful, eye-catching, and a little hard to manage at times. If you think about it, every strand is like a shout-out to your uniqueness. So, if someone calls you "fire-engine" or asks if you've been rolling in a bag of Cheetos, just flash a grin and own it. After all, they're the ones who will spend the rest of their lives blending in with their boring brown or basic blonde. You? You're a walking masterpiece, a dazzling work of art that could even make Picasso a bit jealous.

Next, let's talk about the inevitable comparisons. Yes, redheads have often been portrayed as fiery, feisty, and sometimes a little too intense for their own good—think of all the times you've heard, "Wow, you must be a handful!" Spoiler alert: we are! But remember, it's not a curse; it's a superpower! Channel that fierceness into your passions, whether that's art, sports, or even mastering the perfect TikTok dance. Just be prepared for the occasional eye-roll when someone assumes your enthusiasm is just a byproduct of your hair color. "No, Karen, I'm not just fiery because of my hair; I'm also really into gardening!" (Trust me, your future self will appreciate those unexpected green thumb skills.)

Now, let's address the elephant in the room: sunburns. For us redheads, the sun can sometimes feel like that friend who shows up uninvited to every party. "Oh, you thought you'd enjoy a lovely day at the beach? Surprise! Here's a sunburn that will make you look like a boiled lobster!" The key here is to embrace the art of sunscreen application. Consider it a ritual. Lather it on like you're frosting a cake—thick and generous! And don't forget that wide-brimmed hat. You'll not only protect your fair skin but also look fabulously mysterious, like a sun-kissed siren ready to take on the world.

For those moments when you might face a little jealousy or teasing from non-redheads, remember this: they're often just envious of your fabulousness. After all, we redheads are like the exclusive club that everyone wants to join, but very few can. So, when someone makes a snarky comment about your hair, respond with a wink and a clever retort. "Jealousy is just admiration in disguise, darling!" This way, you'll leave them stunned, pondering the meaning of life while you strut away like the superstar you are.

As you navigate the world of being a redhead, surround yourself with a supportive crew. Find your fellow fiery-haired friends or allies who understand the struggles of finding the right shade of red lipstick or the art of using dry shampoo (because let's be honest, some days, we need all the help we can get). Together, you can celebrate your uniqueness and share in the hilarity of your collective experiences. Plus, who wouldn't want to commiserate over that one time you accidentally bought a bright orange sweater thinking it was "red"? Spoiler alert: it was not, and now you resemble a traffic cone.

Lastly, always remember that your red hair is just one part of your fabulous self. While it's a defining feature, it doesn't solely define you. Embrace your passions, quirks, and interests—be it reading, sports, or a borderline obsession with collecting rubber ducks. You are a complex, multifaceted individual, and your hair is just the icing on the cake (or should I say, the cherry on top?). So, go out there and show the world the vibrant personality that comes with those stunning red tresses!

In closing, dear young redheads, being a redhead is a journey filled with ups, downs, and a whole lot of fabulousness. Embrace your identity with humor and pride. Wear your hair like a crown, and let your personality shine even brighter. You are part of a unique lineage that has shaped history, culture, and society in ways you may not even realize. So, step confidently into the world, and remember: red is not just a hair color; it's a lifestyle!

A Life on Fire

Being a redhead is more than just a hair color; it's a badge of honor, a signal flare, and often a conversation starter that can lead to both delightful and bewildering interactions. As we reflect on what it truly means to be a redhead, we find ourselves embracing not just the fiery hue of our hair but also the vibrant spirit that comes along with it.

Let's face it: red hair often feels like a living, breathing entity. It demands attention like a diva at a concert. Whether it's the instant recognition when you enter a room or the inquisitive stares from strangers who seem convinced they've just spotted a unicorn, being a redhead is like having a personal spotlight that follows you everywhere. And while it can be exhausting, it also offers a certain kind of power—an ability to turn heads, spark conversations, and make people smile (or sometimes cringe).

In our reflections, we can't overlook the unique challenges that come with this fiery identity. For one, the sheer number of assumptions people make about us can be staggering. We've all heard the cliché: "Redheads must have fiery tempers!" Sure, we might have a passion for things, whether it's advocating for a cause or passionately debating the best pizza toppings. But to imply that we're all just walking, talking drama queens? Come on! It's a little reductive, much like saying all blondes are ditzy or all brunettes are boring.

Yet, in these assumptions lies an opportunity to educate. By embracing our individuality, we can shatter stereotypes, one fiery comment at a time. The next time someone insists you must be a handful, you can simply respond, "Yes, but it's a handful of fabulous!"

Embracing our identity as redheads means celebrating our differences, but it also means recognizing the beauty in diversity among all hair colors, styles, and personalities. After all, variety is what makes life interesting! In a world full of brown, black, and blonde, our vibrant locks stand out like a bold piece of abstract art. And that's something to celebrate!

As we ponder the journey of being a redhead, we realize that it often mirrors our experiences of individuality. We might share a common hair color, but our stories are uniquely our own. Each redhead carries a history, a personality, and a way of navigating the world that is entirely distinct. Some may thrive in the spotlight, while others prefer a more subtle approach. And that's perfectly okay!

So, how do we celebrate these differences? First, we can share our stories. Whether through social media, community gatherings, or casual chats over coffee, the redhead community is a tapestry of experiences waiting to be unraveled. Each tale of triumph, humor, or even the occasional mishap adds to the richness of our collective identity.

Next, we should uplift one another. Let's ditch the petty rivalries and embrace the camaraderie that comes with being part of this unique club. Encourage one another to stand out, be bold, and live authentically. Compliment that fiery red lip color, cheer on the red-haired friend who just took a daring leap into the world of fashion, or simply laugh together at the absurdity of being asked if you've "ever met a leprechaun."

Being a redhead is about more than just the hair; it's about embracing the passionate spirit that comes with it. It's about standing up to stereotypes and being proud of who we are. We're a community filled with humor, fierceness, and a whole lot of love for our uniquely vibrant selves. So let's celebrate our individuality, cherish our differences, and continue to shine brightly in a world that sometimes feels all too gray.

Remember: we are the fire in the world's hair color spectrum, and that fire is something to be celebrated every single day!

One Final Spark

Embracing our uniqueness is a journey we all share, and it's one that transcends hair color. While being a redhead comes with its own set of quirks, eccentricities, and a fiery flair, the essence of celebrating who we are lies in recognizing that everyone has something special to bring to the table—whether you're a blonde, brunette, or rockin' the silver fox look. So, let's take a moment to revel in our differences and the delightful experiences that come with them.

At the heart of this journey is the understanding that our differences make us vibrant. Think about it: we all have traits, quirks, and experiences that shape our identities. Those peculiarities turn the mundane into the extraordinary, much like how a splash of hot sauce can transform a bland meal into a culinary fiesta. Whether you're the life of the party with your fiery locks or you prefer a more understated approach, remember: your uniqueness is your superpower!

Imagine walking into a room filled with people, and instead of blending into the background, you shine bright like a diamond—or a dazzling ruby, if we're sticking to the color theme! That's the power of embracing who you are. It's about owning your individuality, quirks, and all. Maybe you have a penchant for knitting cozy sweaters for your cat, or perhaps you can quote every line from your favorite movie. Whatever it is, wear it like a badge of honor! You might even start a trend: "Witty Movie Quote Enthusiast" could be the next big thing!

And speaking of trends, let's not forget how the world seems to have a knack for gravitating toward the unusual. Remember the "No Poo" hair movement? That's right, while some of us were frantically searching for the best shampoo, others were reveling in their au naturel locks. So if your unique traits make you feel like the eccentric star of a quirky indie film, embrace it! You're not just a character; you're the lead in your own spectacular story.

As we encourage one another to embrace our uniqueness, let's also create space for shared experiences. This is where you come in! We want to hear your stories—whether you've faced the world with confidence or learned to love those peculiar traits that set you apart. Have you had an encounter that made you laugh, cry, or just shake your head in disbelief? Perhaps you were the only one in the room who dared to wear polka dots with stripes, and instead of getting a side-eye, you sparked a fashion revolution! Or maybe you accidentally turned a casual outing into an impromptu stand-up routine.

We invite you to share your redhead experiences (or any uniquely you experiences!) with us. Feel free to drop us an email at MandolinPublishing@gmail.com. Your stories—whether they're hilarious, heartwarming, or downright ridiculous—will add to our community narrative. Together, we can create a mosaic of experiences that celebrates the colorful array of humanity. Think of it as a collective diary where we can all contribute our most ridiculous moments and laugh together.

Remember, each time you embrace your uniqueness, you inspire others to do the same. You become a beacon of light for those still finding their way. And let's be honest, sometimes it can be tough out there. We've all had moments where we felt like we were wearing a sign that read "Look at me, I'm different!" But instead of shrinking away, let's stand tall, toss our hair (or flaunt our bold hats), and say, "Yes, I am fabulous, and you can't dim my shine!"

In the end, whether you're a fiery redhead or a classic brunette, let's take a moment to celebrate our quirks, laugh at our foibles, and revel in the beautiful diversity that makes life so incredibly rich. Life is too short to hide in the shadows, so let's embrace who we are—because the world needs more of your unique light!

So, dear reader, as we navigate this wild adventure called life, remember: your individuality is not just a trait; it's a treasure. The more you embrace it, the more vibrant your world becomes. So let's continue to shine, support one another, and share in the joy of being unapologetically ourselves. After all, the world is a much more colorful place with all of us being our authentic selves!

Don't forget!

You can leave a review for free at whatever online book outlet you like! It's like sending a cookie to the author without spending a dime—no calories, no crumbs, and no risk of your cat stealing it! Just a sweet little note that says, "Hey, I liked your book!" instead of "I brought you a snack that's now a cat toy."